SERGE DEDINA

SURFING THE BORDER

Adventures at the Edge of the Ocean

Surfing the Border: Adventures at the Edge of the Ocean

WILDCOAST
©2015 WILDCOAST
All rights reserved. First edition.

Cover and book design by Cathy Klein
Printed in the United States of America.

Please direct comments and inquiries to:
WILDCOAST
925 Seacoast Drive
Imperial Beach, CA 91932
619.423.8665 ext. 200
info@wildcoast.net
www.wildcoast.net

18 17 16 15   4 3 2 1

Library of Congress Control Number: 2014959204

Contents

Part III Travel

Acknowledgements

This book would not have been possible with out the hospitality and support of my colleagues, friends, and family in Imperial Beach, Baja, and around the world. First and foremost I am grateful to my awesome staff and board at WILDCOAST/COSTASALVAJE. Zach Plopper, Eduardo Najera, Sofia Gomez, Cesar Garcia, Sergio Flores, Natalia Parra, Cecilia Fischer, Ben McCue, and Fay Crevoshay accompanied me in the field. Thanks also to the generous donors who make my work at WILDCOAST possible.

Fellow surf dads Daren Johnson, Beto Bedolfe, Mike Hastings, Robert Stabenow, Dwayne Fernandez, Greg Tate, Dave Lopez, Mark West, Andrew Aldredge, Chris Patterson, and Jeff and Jim Knox never fail to provide moral support and continuous advice on staying sane while raising rambunctious and high-energy teenage surfers.

In Baja California, thanks to Aida Navarro, Fernando Ochoa, Mike Vargas, Gustavo Danemann, Octavio Aburto, Kimball Taylor, Benito Bermudez, Alfonso Aguirre, Jim Pickell, the Castro family, the Merrill family in Todos Santos, the Johnson family, Dawn Pier, Joan Hafenecker, Dick Russell and everyone at El Faro, Javier Villavicencio, the Aguilar and Mayoral families, Isidro Arce, Pulga Murillo, Jim and Judy Tolbert of Baja Books, Jaime Morales, Alfredo Ramirez, and the members of the Red Costasalvaje. I am indebted to Javier Plascencia of Misión 19 and Finca Altozano, Javier Martinez of Boules, and David Martinez of Muelle 3 for sharing their food and vision of a new path for Baja.

In mainland Mexico, I am grateful for the hospitality and friendship of Homero and Betty Aridjis; Darrin and Paulina Polischuk; Araceli Oregon and the residents of Barra de Potosi; Lainie and Mike Johnstone; Paul Van Vleck; Ernesto "Pato" Leon Sandoval; Sergio and Natalia Flores; Kristy Murphy and Cat Slatinsky of Siren Surf Adventures; Lourdes of Saladita; Pablo Narvaez; Guillermo "Memo" Gonzalez of the Morro Ayuta Sea Turtle Center; and Manuel Rodriguez of the National Mexican Turtle Center in Mazunte.

My trips to Europe would not have been possible without the help of my family in England and France, who have embraced surfing and the sea. I am grateful to the organizers of the Pacific Rim Whale Festival in Tofino for their hospitality and introducing me to such a cool and beautiful corner of the surfing world. Australians are about the nicest people on the planet, and wherever we went the boys and I were treated with kindness and generosity.

Thanks to Jim Moriarty and Chad Nelsen of the Surfrider Foundation; Nik Strong-Cvetich, Dean LaTourrette and Will Henry of Save the Waves; Hugo Tagholm and Andy Cummins of Surfers Against Sewage; and all the members of the Global Wave Coalition for their dedication to saving waves. My swim team—Mike Martino, Patti and Ken Ireland, Rene Murphy, Alberto Garza, and Mike Keeney—motivate me to do better or at least try to. And thanks to Khari Johnson, Barbara Bry, and Chris Jennewein for providing an outlet for these stories. Thanks to Matt Warshaw for fact-checking assistance and Dana Link-Herrera, Cathy Klein, Debi Young, and Linda Scott and her team at eFrog Press for their editorial and production support.

My sons, Israel and Daniel, inspire me to keep surfing and see the world with open eyes. My wife, Emily, has shared adventures with me for more than thirty years. She never tires of the joy of experiencing something new. Thank you all.

Introduction

THE RETURN OF STOKE

There is not a more iconic restaurant along the Transpeninsular Highway in Baja California than Mama Espinoza's in El Rosario. Covered in off-road and surf stickers, Mama Espinoza's is a required Baja pit stop for surfers, Baja 1000 crews, and sportfishermen.

For a few years after 2007, restaurants like Mama Espinoza's had very few visitors. That is when a series of robberies of surfers and off-roaders occurred in Baja, and Americans literally stopped traveling south of the border. Pretty soon the entire peninsula emptied of tourists. While that was great for the few remaining surfers who ignored very real security issues to catch the latest swell, it was a crisis for anyone in Baja's tourism industry.

So I was surprised when I stopped into Mama Espinoza's for dinner in November 2010, on a trip to the Pacific coast of central Baja, and found the restaurant packed with tourists. There were Baja 1000 pre-run crews fueling up after a long day eating dust. Sunburned sportfishermen on their way home from Bahía de los Ángeles downed Pacificos. I was elated to see that Baja was finally back from the brink of crisis.

This book represents that period after 2010 when Mexico emerged from its recessionary and narco war shell. In Baja California, thanks to a new generation of entrepreneurs, chefs, vintners, and hoteliers, a new tourism scene developed that is rooted in the flavors and cultures of both land and sea. It was a development that I could never have predicted given the depth of the collapse of Baja's tourism economy in 2007.

Tijuana chefs Javier Plascencia and Miguel Angel Guerrero, along with their colleagues in the Guadalupe Valley and Ensenada such as Diego Hernandez, Javier and David Martinez, Benito Molina, and Solange Muris, used the recession to create an extraordinarily unique food and wine scene that provided even die-hard Baja know-it-alls like me with something new and exciting to discover. Best of all, they created a new tourism model based on sustainably working with and for the conservation of local landscapes rather than destroying them.

Part I is autobiographical. It includes essays on how I started surfing in the blue-collar border beach town of Imperial Beach. The experiences of my parents during World War II ultimately led them to my peculiar corner of North America, which resulted in my growing up and eventually working on both sides of the US-Mexico border. For me, the border is a physical barrier that cuts through a distinctly unique region where people share waves, food, family, art, music, and friendship regardless of the state of relations between Mexico City and Washington, D.C.

In Part II, I delve into surf culture, which due to the Great Recession also faced its own reckoning and retrenchment. My own experience as a surf dad, in which I introduced my two sons to the surf culture that captivated me as a teenager, helped me to reexplore cultural terrain that I had almost given up on. I also discuss some of the environmental issues including climate change, sea level rise, sand replenishment, and protecting surf spots as reserves that surfers are now grappling with.

In Part III, I share stories of my travels, in which I attempt to transcend boundaries and find the original and unique among our increasingly crowded and homogeneous world. Whether in my hometown of Imperial Beach, just north of the US-Mexico border;

exploring the mangroves and points of Guerrero and Oaxaca in southern Mexico; or enjoying the verdant coastlines of Europe, Canada, and Australia, I explored regional cultures, food, natural beauty, and waves.

I got my feet wet as a traveler when my parents dragged my little brother, Nicky, and me around Mexico and Central America in our 1974 green Ford Econoline van. We lived in El Salvador for a year and camped everywhere. My family and I explored ancient ruins and white sand beaches. Our van got stuck in hideous jungle mud and we visited wild national parks where my little brother and I were delighted to be close to monkeys and giant iguanas up close.

That year in Mexico and Central America as a ten-year-old whet my appetite for adventure. I later lived and surfed in Europe, Morocco, Mexico, and Costa Rica. I met my wife, Emily, on a university year-abroad program in Peru and together we traveled around South America. Later during grad school we lived in Baja for two years. After our sons were born, I wanted to share those same experiences. So Emily, Israel, Daniel, and I explored wave-rich regions of Australia, New Zealand, Mexico, and Europe. Our voyages were more than just about surfing. I am as big a fan of visiting national parks and cultural treasures as I am of finding perfect waves.

For me, surfing is more than just riding waves. The unique view of surfers as outsiders on the edge of civilization provides an opportunity to experience life beyond borders and find the increasingly disappearing natural and cultural niches that remain.

PART I

Surfing the Border

" They seemed content to leave the Tijuana River Valley to the park rangers and Border Patrol, to the assorted cowboys, truck farmers, Indians, environmentalists, drug runners or bandidos, and burro eaters... "

—Kem Nunn, *Tijuana Straits*

Chapter 1

SURFING WITH THE HULK

In the summer of 1977, I was thirteen and desperately wanted to be a surfer. A neighbor, Harry Hildebrand, introduced me to Radical Roy, who had a board for sale. Roy, who knee-paddled, rode switchfoot, and only surfed the north side of the Imperial Beach Pier, hooked me up with a 6'11", no-name winger-rounded pin single fin for thirteen dollars. Harry then sold me a beavertail wet suit for four dollars and I was set.

With my board under my arm, I rode my Schwinn ten-speed two miles from my house on Hemlock Avenue to the north side of the pier. I immediately met twelve-year-old Donny Dominguez who had a Gerry Lopez-style bowl haircut and knew way more about surfing and girls than I did. Donny was also was the proud owner of an electric purple pintail shaped by Richard Jolie.

"Jolie shaped the board in Hawaii," said Donny. "He's the man."

"That's cool," I replied, even though I had no idea why it was cool or why it mattered that Jolie lived and shaped in Hawaii.

Over the summer, Donny and I met at the beach each morning, surfed all day, and checked out girls from the safety of our towels. We stayed away from the older guys who hung out at the end of Elm Avenue. Donny and I were sure they would steal our boards or bikes.

When Mar Vista Junior High started that September, I was no

longer a goofy, long-haired seventh grader who wore Levi's cut-offs and committed the sin of pairing white Converse high-tops with black socks. I was a surfer, which I prayed would make me a little cooler.

I hung out with Donny, Tim Sweeney, Dan Mehlos, Brian Sargent, John Arnold, Larry Crauswell, Bobby Maupin, Tim Hannan, and Greg Paarman. We spent our days skateboarding, riding our bikes to the beach, and surfing. Imperial Beach back then was a tough place for a teenager. On campus I was mostly concerned with avoiding the Imperial gang members who wore chino pants and white T-shirts, and had their hair greased back or trained to stay in place with hairnets.

The Imperials often fought the IB Locals, who had long hair, wore Levi's and white T-shirts, had an affinity for Led Zeppelin, Deep Purple, and Jimi Hendrix, and smoked a lot of pot. Sometimes the divisions between the two groups divided families. Rafe, an IB Local, used to fight his twin brother, Roberto, an Imperial, on the gum-stained junior high playground before PE roll call. When a fight between the twins erupted, I prayed it wouldn't turn into a gang melee that I would be caught in. I had no desire to get my ass kicked by a guy wearing a hairnet.

The Imperial Beach Pier was to be avoided at all costs. That is where mean and tough bikers hung out and where a parade of wild-eyed babbling crazy people might jump me. If I was lucky, the nightly congregation of drunks and drug addicts who spent the night partying around the fire rings by the pier would be passed out by the time I arrived at the beach at dawn to surf.

Some of my friends did not escape the drugs that were everywhere. One of my long-haired and perpetually sunburned friends was a prototype Joel Tudor long before the resurgence of longboarding. He took too much LSD and ended up wearing a paper sack over his head with eyeholes cut out when he surfed. Then he disappeared.

Because none of us had any cash and our parents rarely gave us any, my friends and I were always scrambling for ways to earn money to buy surfboards and wet suits. Tim Hannan and I decided to go into the surf wax business. We bought a giant purple square foot candle from the local Goodwill and borrowed muffin pans from Lona, Tim's mom. I put the candle on the Ping-Pong table in our garage and hacked it up with a machete.

Tim and I picked up the pieces of candle spread out over the floor, shoved the wax into the muffin holes, and tossed the pan in the oven to bake our surf wax.

"We're going to make a bunch of money from this," said Tim.

"Yeah," I replied. "This is going to be awesome."

We later hawked the purple misshapen lumps we pried out of the muffin pans at R.C.'s Surflines, a surf shop on Palm Avenue and Second Street. The guys hanging out at the shop laughed at us when we walked in with our new product.

"You kooks," they all said in unison as we feebly showed Joe Ellis, who ran the shop, our paper sack of mangled candle wax.

"Are you kidding me?" said Joe, who was an engineering student at Cal Poly Pomona. "Get out of here."

————

Back then no one had a clue when waves were coming, since there was no such thing as surf forecasting like there is today. We just showed up at the beach each morning and hoped for the best.

On the Sunday of Labor Day weekend in 1978, I bicycled to the pier and found Tim Hannan waiting for me. He was slack-jawed at the sight of empty eight-foot hurricane-fueled cylinders reeling off the pier for two hundred yards. We didn't know that Hurricane Norman was spinning off the coast in Baja and slowly moving toward Southern California.

"It's too big to paddle out," said Tim, a fiery redheaded

kneeboarder who was up for anything.

"We could jump off the pier," I said, even though I dreaded the idea. I had avoided jumping off the pier all winter.

"Okay," said Tim. "That will be great."

While I watched giant sets pound the beach, Tim locked up our bikes to a light pole. We waxed our surfboards and took the long walk past the open white lifeguard box that spanned the middle of the pier. About twenty yards past the box, we stopped and looked over the railing.

"Let's throw our stuff off here," said Tim.

I let Tim jump first. He chucked his Craig kneeboard off the pier, stood on the pier railing, and jumped in the water more than twenty feet below with his green Churchill swim fins in his hands.

After Tim plopped into the water, he sprang up and yelled, "Come on, pussy. Jump in!"

I threw my board into the water below and leapt off the railing. It took forever to hit the water. The ocean smacked my butt hard. I swam over to my board, attached my leash to my right leg, and paddled over to where Tim sat laughing at me.

"You wuss," he said. "You were shitting your pants."

I paddled behind Tim as we made our way to the lineup while watching gnarly lefts way beyond my ability break off the pier. The only other person out was a tough-looking older guy with brown hair and a mustache. He wore yellow surf trunks and a raggedy, faded Incredible Hulk T-shirt.

"That's the Hulk," said Tim. "Stay away from him. He's a badass."

I had heard stories about Danny "Hulk" Bussell. He was the toughest surfer in town and was rumored to have beaten up a guy who jumped him from a staircase and stabbed him in the back. I owned a 7'10" Incredible Hulk diamond tail single fin with a weight in the nose I had bought at a garage sale for five dollars. Shaped by Mike "Electric Duck" Richardson, it had a picture of the Hulk on the nose. The fishing weight was designed to aid in paddling into offshore waves at the Tijuana Sloughs.

"The Hulk surfed huge waves on the North Shore," said Tim. Because his dad played beach volleyball and he had two older sisters, Patti and Kathy, who were in high school and were friends with all the cool older surfers, Tim knew everything.

A humongous wave pushed through the pier, creating a hollow wedging bowl. The Hulk calmly paddled into the wave behind the peak. He made a hairball backside bottom turn, turned into the barrel, and flew down the wave toward the decaying hotel down the beach.

"Did you see that?" I said. "That guy is radical."

A few minutes later, the Hulk paddled back to the pier and grunted hello to Tim and me. He continued taking off on big gnarly waves behind the peak. I managed to catch a few set waves. Later on the beach I felt pretty good about surviving those terrifying waves.

A little over a year and a half later, a giant winter swell destroyed the end of the pier. The Hulk died a few years later. To this day, I've never seen anyone surf with more confidence, aggression, and finesse than Danny "Hulk" Bussell. As for me, nothing could ever top surfing a hurricane swell with the scariest and most badass surfer on the coast.

Chapter 2

SURF MUM

My first memories are of the beach with my mother, or "mum." Born in London just before World War II, Mum never lost the joy of spending a day by the sea. "For me, the seaside in California was like seeing oranges on trees. It was something so out of place in my life," she said.

My mother's pleasure in our California coast was the result of living in London during WWII, where routine German bombing raids made enjoying the seaside impossible.

"Back then, many people lived in London till they died and never saw a beach. We never went to the beach during the war," she said. "Even after the war there was barbed wire all over the beaches in Cornwall.

"I remember during the war my father holding me while we watched an aerial dogfight between the RAF and the Germans. My dad said, 'Take a look at this because you won't see this again.' When the bombs came, we went to a shelter that had beds on each side. You could hear the sound of the bombers coming over and all of a sudden it stopped and everyone waited and my dad said, 'Some other poor buggers got it.'"

The joyous routines of childhood during the Blitz often turned to tragedy. "I remember children queuing up for ice cream in our neighborhood and they all were bombed. More than twenty died."

Later my grandmother Dolly was caught at home when a bomb hit. "The entire house collapsed. But your grandmother hid under the portable metal bomb shelter in the dining room. My father came home from work to the rescue crews going through the house and they found her."

Mum's first trip to the coast was after the war. "Pop, my sister's father-in-law, took my sister Jill and me to the seaside in a big beautiful car. On the way there we saw castles and then Pop pulled off the road to stop. In the distance, we could see this big shimmering pool and Pop said it was the sea. We were so excited when we arrived and could make sandcastles."

In the 1950s, my mother met my father, a French-American serviceman, in London. Later they married and ended up moving west to Los Angeles.

When I was a child during the mid to late 1960s, Mother would take me to the beach to bake me in the sun. She always had a picnic basket ready with cold roast chicken, French bread, homemade mayonnaise, and fresh fruit.

"We went to the beach almost everyday at either Venice, Santa Monica, and Malibu," she recalled. "Back in those days, people used to think I was crazy to take you to the beach in the winter. But the weather in LA compared to England was lovely."

When we moved to Imperial Beach, Mother led our family and neighborhood children to the mouth of the Tijuana Estuary for all-day picnics among the dunes. Enamored of the beauty of our backyard habitat, Mother became involved in efforts to preserve it.

In 1974, our family spent a year in El Salvador. We camped at tropical beaches throughout Mexico and Central America. I never tired of exploring jungle ruins, watching monkeys in the rainforest, or carefully walking through old passageways of Mayan ruins with my little brother.

After we returned to Imperial Beach, I started surfing at the age of thirteen. "I never imagined seeing my son with a surfboard," Mum said.

Mum once took my friends and me on a surf trip to northern Baja in our 1964 VW van. While we surfed K-38, she cooked up pancakes in the dirt parking lot. The only downside to surfing, as my proper English mother once told me, was our language. "You and your friends sounded idiotic talking about surfing. I used to think, 'What happened to my formerly intelligent oldest son?'"

Josephine with Nick, Carlsbad State Park, 1969

My mother, Josephine Alexandria Fournier Dedina, retired from her career as an attorney and judge pro tem a few years ago to enjoy her three grandchildren. She now has terminal cancer.

In the afternoons after work, I sit with my mum at her home near the sloughs. We drink cups of tea and talk about when my brother and I were little, and how my mother opened a magical doorway to a lovely life filled with sunny beach days.

I will never forget that the best days of my life and hers were spent in the company of our family, at the seaside.

———

My mother passed away in February 2011.

Chapter 3
SURF DAD

There was never a time when my father, an immigrant who came to America from France to escape the Nazi occupation of Europe, wasn't loading up our Ford station wagon and taking us to the beach.

In 1939, at the age of six, my father came to the United States from France with my grandma Lotti and his brother, Roland.

"In France as a little tyke, I played on a beach covered by pebbles and round pieces of wine bottles rounded by the surf," my dad, Michel Dedina, recalled from his home near the Tijuana Estuary in Imperial Beach.

"I was scared when we came to America because my big brother, Roland, told me America had skyscrapers and one would collapse on me," he said. "In New York we visited the beach at Coney Island. It was crowded. Wall-to-wall people. But there was great corn on the cob."

After the war my father moved back to Paris. Some of his family had been sent to concentration camps or killed by the Gestapo. "Everyone was tired of the war and nobody wanted to talk about air raids, combat, and concentration camps. There were no medals for those who suffered," he said.

Later my father joined the American air force during the Korean

War and met my mother in London while he was stationed in England. They married in New York City, where my father published two novels. Mom and Dad eventually made their way to California and settled in Los Angeles. "Your mom and I had visited and liked California. Liked the beach, but found the water cold," said Dad.

My parents never camped in Europe but discovered the value of outings at California state parks. On our first camping trip in the late 1960s, we pitched a borrowed Korean War-era military surplus tent at Carlsbad State Beach.

Mom and Dad were cold and miserable in their homemade sleeping bags stitched together from old blankets. My little brother, Nicky, and I were in heaven and never wanted the trip to end.

We lugged that tent up and down the coast of California, giving rides to hitchhiking hippies while enjoying coastal campgrounds from San Diego to Big Sur. In 1971 we moved to Imperial Beach, where life revolved around weekends at the beach and traipsing around the Tijuana Estuary.

Meanwhile, Dad earned his master's degree in television and film at SDSU, where he studied with Desi Arnaz. After grad school, Dad purchased a 1974 Ford Econoline van, loaded it up with camping gear and our clothes, and drove us south to El Salvador. Dad had a job with the US Agency for International Development.

"I should have been more scared than I was during our trip," he recalled. "We had to deal with crooked customs and immigration officers. I learned to pay the bribes. There were more honest officers than crooks."

It was during our year in El Salvador that I wanted to be a surfer. The visiting Californians strolling down the beach with their surfboards looked incredibly cool. I wanted to be like them. That year we camped on white sand beaches and explored indigenous villages and ancient ruins in Guatemala, Chiapas, Yucatán, Quintana Roo, and Belize.

I started surfing after our return to Imperial Beach and convinced Dad to take my friends and me to Baja. There we surfed perfect point waves while Dad cooked up spaghetti with lobster sauce.

In the early 1990s, when my wife Emily and I lived in Baja's San Ignacio Lagoon to study gray whales, Dad drove down with my mother to visit. Dad was in heaven when the local fishermen called him "Don Miguel."

Michel with Nick and Serge, Guatemala, 1974

"I've been waiting my entire life to be called Don Miguel," he said.

After Israel and Daniel were born, Dad foraged the streets for old surfboards and wet suits and took our kids to the beach to surf.

"I stood Daniel on a wide, long surfboard on tiny waves," said my father. "He surfed and remained standing. A guy came over and asked, 'Who is that kid?' Nonchalantly, I replied, 'My grandson.' The guy asked, 'How old is he?' I replied, 'Four.' The guy said, 'Wow. Four years old.'"

Despite a good life in America, Dad never forgot what the Nazis and their French collaborators had stolen from his family. He applied for a settlement from the French Commission for the Compensation of Victims of Spoliation Resulting from Anti-Semitic Legislation in Force During the Occupation.

"I could not have lived with myself if I had not tried to fight for what we had lost. The first verdict was against us. So we appealed. I went to the appeals tribunal in Paris. There were five judges, one of whom it turned out was against us when they deliberated some weeks later. I can only guess why or how we won."

At the tribunal, Dad's cousin Lisette corroborated my father's testimony. The Nazis murdered her parents. Her brother, Bernard Fall, fought in the Resistance and later worked at the Nuremberg Trials. "Our award was small, which was shared with Roland's family. It wasn't about the money."

After more than fifty years of marriage, Dad lost my mother to cancer a few years back. Today, at the age of eighty, he maneuvers his three-wheel electric bicycle around Imperial Beach and religiously attends the surf competitions, water polo games, and swim meets of his grandsons. He also enjoys long visits with my brother, Nick, and his family in San Francisco.

Dad occasionally speaks out at local city council meetings about preserving local beaches and parks.

I owe my sense of adventure to my father, along with my determination to never waiver in the pursuit of justice. After all, that is what my father taught me being an American means.

Chapter 4
SURFING THE BORDER

On a sunny Sunday morning, I paddled my surfboard next to the algae-covered metal border fence at Border Field State Park that divides California from Mexico. As I caught a wave, I thought back to the first time my father brought me here when I was seven years old.

Back then, Border Field was a dusty lot laid out around a carved marble boundary marker inaugurated by Pat Nixon. Today, the park is under continual surveillance by the Border Patrol and is located next to a bullring in Playas de Tijuana, a wealthy Tijuana suburb. To the north, across a large expanse of salt marsh known locally as the sloughs, is my blue-collar hometown of Imperial Beach. The sloughs were the focal point of my childhood that was a mix of beach and border.

For my father, Border Field was a reminder that for our family, borders were obstacles to be jumped, bypassed, and ignored. Nationality was meaningless and fluid, determined by whatever it took to avoid arrest by a *gendarme* after being ratted out by an evil *concierge*.

By moving to Imperial Beach, a town far removed from the paisley fantasia of coastal Southern California, my dad had inadvertently surrounded himself with the reminders of his own journey to America.

Just about every night, our neighborhood of low-rent stucco apartments and houses— located a few blocks from the Tijuana River Valley—was overrun by hundreds of Mexican refugees fleeing poverty, violence, and the Border Patrol helicopters and trucks that chased them. When the migrants jumped our fence to hide in the backyard or in the garage, my father patiently, wordlessly, and without fear unlocked our side gate or opened the garage door and let them go.

My father often told me that he kept the back door of our house unlocked in case we had to flee in the middle of the night if the police ever came to round us up. I often wondered where we would go. Would we run to Mexico? Would I end up like the Mexican kid who stumbled across our campfire in the sloughs after my dad had inexplicably decided to have a family campout in the middle of the Border Patrol's nightly war zone?

That skinny boy—hungry, scared, and alone—woke me up from the safety of my sleeping bag set in the sand by the fire.

"How far is San Francisco?" he asked.

"Not too far to the north," my dad replied in his broken Spanish, not wanting to curtail the boy's dream with the reality of the long trail ahead.

———

I'm not sure what my father thought of the bearded, shirtless bikers, some with large swastika arm tattoos, who hung out on the Imperial Beach Pier. One of them, Dave, was the son of our neighbor Rose, a little old lady who hailed from the South. Dave, who had just been released from prison on a manslaughter charge, spent weekends with his friends working on their choppers in Rose's driveway.

Once, when Mom lost my little brother, Nicky, at the beach, she ran across Dave in the pier parking lot. Dave quickly organized a search for my brother with his biker buddies. They found Nicky, but pleasant neighborly feelings didn't last long when Dave's younger brother Larry pulled a knife on my mother.

My mother did not spend much time worrying about Larry and his knife. She cheerily led Nicky, the neighborhood kids, and me down to the sloughs on our bikes to spend the day clamming and bodysurfing.

Back then the Border Patrol did not stop the residents of Tijuana from walking north to spend the day in the Tijuana Estuary. So our family often shared Pismo clam cocktails in the sloughs with Mexican families.

Later after I learned to surf, I worked as an ocean lifeguard. Once I was called to respond to the bloated bodies of two teenagers who self-deported themselves into the ocean near the sloughs, and drowned rather than face arrest by the Border Patrol.

While I watched over swimmers at the beach and the daily parade of migrants walking north, my father rambled through the trails of the sloughs collecting the discarded clothes and documents of the migrants who crossed the salt marsh at night. One morning, after a walk through the sloughs, Dad showed me a passport of a man from El Salvador.

After a winter storm caused flooding in the Tijuana River, I organized a community cleanup to remove storm debris left in the sloughs. At a potluck afterward at an old fire station, my friend Chris and I listened to a man and his friend sing and play the guitar. We were fifteen years old, had just cleaned up a major garbage pile in the sloughs, and felt pretty good.

All a sudden, two bikers I recognized from the pier walked over to our little group. I sensed they had not come to join us in song.

"Hey nigger, get the hell out of here," the taller of the two men yelled at the African-American guitar player.

"Why don't you get the hell out of here," responded the friend, a short white man wearing a Greek fisherman's cap.

Border Field State Park

Without saying anything, the tall biker took out a pistol from his pants and shot the guitar player's friend in the mouth. Chris and I ran and jumped over a fence to get away.

No one cared much about the racist shooting. Later when I thought about it, I found it odd that it was safer to spend the night camping in the sloughs—among the refugees who swarmed it each night—than celebrating its cleanup in town.

On the morning I surfed Border Field a couple of years ago, my son Israel and my friend Chris—who witnessed the shooting with me decades ago—accompanied me. After surfing for a bit, I left the water and walked over to the border fence.

A man approached me from the Mexican side. His three-year-old daughter held his hand and a raggedy blonde Barbie. For a moment, we stared at each other through the slots in the metal barrier. "There didn't used to be a fence here when I was a kid," I said.

We both smiled and looked toward the ocean where Israel surfed a wave a few feet from the large sign with big red letters stuck to the end of the border fence that read "Danger-Peligro."

PART II

Surf Culture and Environment

" "Okay. I get it. This is where you tell me that 'locals rule,' and that yuppie insects like me shouldn't be surfing the break, right?" "

—Keanu Reeves as Johnny Utah in *Point Break*

Chapter 5

RAISING GROMS: A GUIDE TO THE CARE AND FEEDING OF KID SURFERS

While many surfers consider raising groms, until you are immersed in this lifelong activity, you might not realize the responsibilities and challenges that await you. Here are some tips to help surf parents manage this laborious, costly, and time-intensive process.

Groms are expensive. After you feed them they grow quickly out of wet suits, surfboards, board shorts, and shoes. Due to the high cost of boards and wet suits, it is imperative that you train the groms to fund their own surfing expenses.

As soon as the groms can walk, take them to the beach and teach them to search garbage cans for leftover redemption bottles and cans. You can also make the rounds in your neighborhood to search for discarded boards and wet suits. There is no need to purchase new gear when you can scrounge from the street.

Groms need to swim well. Very well. If the groms want to surf with you they should be physically prepared. Swim teams, water polo, and junior lifeguard programs should follow extensive swim lessons. Ocean-safe groms make for happy parents and lifeguards.

Parents should become as proficient in ding repair as possible.

That is because as soon your groms learn to surf, they will return from the beach with a dinged or broken board. If you lack a garage or workshop, feel free to turn your grom's bedroom into a combo ding repair workshop/bedroom. Just make sure there is plenty of ventilation.

Groms should also learn ding repair. Just remove all carpeting from your home. Groms will track resin and fiberglass (in addition to sand and surf wax) in every nook and cranny of your house. Don't worry. Sand is organic and provides extra nutrients and sodium when mixed with your food.

Consider giving up any other formal hobbies or activities or even a social life that doesn't revolve around surfing. That is because you will be required to drive your groms to the beach and dawn patrol on the weekends or even before school. Consider obtaining your chauffeurs' license as well, since you will be transporting a pack of groms on most of your surf trips.

Groms must be trained to pack surf gear in the car for their entire family. Just don't be surprised to open the car to find your kids waiting inside without having packed anything, or arriving at the beach and having them be surprised that they were expected to pack Mom or Dad's gear, too. Always make sure to check that boards have been strapped to the car properly—or at all.

When they are young, don't expect the groms to get dressed and ready to depart the beach when you are ready to leave. Invariably, they will disappear, only to be found back on the beach eating kelp, rolling around on a dead sea lion, or playing with bird or dog poop.

Feeding groms is the greatest challenge. Groms surf for extended periods of time and forget to eat. They will then complain to their mothers, "Dad starved me," in order to secure a breakfast of homemade pancakes and waffles.

As Mom is ready to serve her own groms, she will be surprised by the plethora of extra hands reaching out to grab whatever she is serving. The extra hands belong to neighboring groms, who were invited over to eat without informing Mom.

During their teen years, groms move in large packs from house to house devouring all available food in fridges and cupboards. This will require you to make several grocery store trips each week. Don't worry; this will only last until they move out of the house. Consider obtaining a second job to pay for your grocery bill.

The groms will eventually surf way better than you do, go off to college, and move away from home. Don't worry. At some point they will get a job (hopefully), marry, and have their own groms. Then you will get to relive the best days of your life by teaching a new generation to love the ocean and surfing as much as you do.

Groms at the Walter Caloca Surf Contest, Ensenada, 2014

Chapter 6

ART AND SOUL AT THE SACRED CRAFT

U pon entering Exhibit Hall at the Del Mar Fairgrounds for the Sacred Craft Consumer Surf Expo, I ran into San Diego surfing pioneers Jack "Woody" Ekstrom of Leucadia and Carl Knox of Carlsbad. I was a friend of big-wave pioneer Dempsey Holder, an old surfing buddy of Woody and Carl. "I surfed with Dempsey back in 1954," said Knox.

Woody's brother, Carl (the brothers grew up down the street from Windansea in La Jolla), an innovative surfboard designer, was honored at the expo in a Tribute to the Masters Shape-Off. The developer of the off-kilter asymmetrical surfboard design, Ekstrom selected esteemed shapers such as Matt Biolos, Tim Bessell, Ryan Burch, George Gall, Wayne Rich, and Daniel Thomson to compete for a $1,000 prize by shaping their own asymmetrical surfboard blanks. Rusty Preisendorfer, Stanley Pleskunas, and Carl himself judged the final products.

"It is like judging art," Ekstrom said. "These guys are like sculptors."

I joined Kevin Stucki of Imperial Beach and his son, Kevin Jr., to observe George Gall of Point Loma's Plus One Surfboards fine-tune his asymmetrical design in a see-through shaping bay.

With more than one hundred and fifty booths representing

surfboard shapers, surf artists, and blank companies, Sacred Craft is all about the surfboard. The economic downturn combined with the threat of mass-manufactured boards in China and Taiwan has made it harder than ever to make a living selling handcrafted surfboards. No one who makes surfboards expects to make much of a profit.

Coronado's Dan Mann was hawking his innovative inCide foam blank with a carbon fiber core. "I just want to help make surfboards better and better," said Mann. "We haven't even scratched the surface of what is possible. For me, the Sacred Craft is a great event. It gets users and manufacturers face-to-face."

"Handcrafted surfboards are a niche market," said Joe Virgilio of Plus One. "Sacred Craft brings the community together."

For the average surfer, Sacred Craft provides an opportunity to catch a glimpse of surfing legends past and present. Big-wave surfer Greg Long autographed posters for a long line of admirers. Mickey Muñoz signed copies of his new book, *No Bad Waves*, at the Patagonia Booth. John Peck, a 1960s surfing stylist, wandered in while I was leaving.

A very popular part of the expo was the Collective Surfboard and Memorabilia Appraisals, a surfing version of the PBS television program *Antiques Roadshow*. I found Imperial Beach surfer Dave Lopez and his teenage son, Loukas, waiting to have a couple of 1970s-era single fins evaluated. Dave was admiring a 1976 7'8" mint-condition Gerry Lopez Lightning Bolt rounded pintail gun that was on exhibition. "That is such a nice board," said Lopez, who spent years surfing the North Shore.

Thomas Meyerhoffer, an innovative and award-winning designer originally from Sweden and now based in Half Moon Bay, had his uniquely shaped surfboards on display.

"I make about one thousand units a year," said Meyerhoffer of his longboards that have a wide point further back than traditional surfboards. "That allows it to feel like a shortboard," Meyerhoffer said.

The Swedish designer doesn't need to shape surfboards to make a living. "Shaping boards allows me to get to do what I love," he said.

Chapter 7

SURFERS GIVING BACK

I t used to be that surfers didn't worry about anything except catching the next wave. For Glen Hening, founder of the Groundswell Society, the 10th Annual Surfing Arts, Science, and Issues Conference (SASIC) was all about surfers moving beyond selfishness and embracing a new spirit of aloha. Cohosted and organized by San Diego State University's new Center for Surf Research, the event brought together more than one hundred and twenty surf industry stalwarts, social entrepreneurs, and everyday surfers to examine the myriad of ways in which surfers can give back.

"The conference confirmed a whole new trend in surfing that's not about commerce or competition, but about community," Hening said. "A university setting, great presentations, honest answers, and a real surf-stoke vibe made SASIC 10 a bit of a milestone."

According to Jess Ponting, director of the Center for Surf Research, the conference marked the beginning of a new era in surfer philanthropy. Originally from Australia, Ponting has carried out research on the economic, ecological, and cultural impacts of surfing tourism in surfing "nirvanas" such as Fiji. During his research, he found that the multimillion-dollar surf tour industry had little impact on alleviating the poverty and environmental degradation of the rural communities that populate many Third World surfing destinations.

In some places that situation is changing. Over the past decade, with the development of organizations such as SurfAid and the emergence of a more strategic form of surf industry philanthropy, a new culture of giving back has emerged among surfers and the surf industry.

Dave Aabo is the founder of Waves for Development, an organization that works to link surfing and community development in the wave-rich coastal desert of northern Peru. At the conference, he provided an overview on how to make a strategic request from a surf company to carry out community work. An ex-Peace Corps volunteer who departed for Peru the day after the conference, Aabo is slowly bringing a more businesslike approach to the complex field of community development.

In a panel on corporate philanthropy, Jeff Wilson of Quiksilver, PJ Connell of Reef, and Derek Sabori of Volcom provided an overview of how their companies make an impact through philanthropy. For all three companies it is critical for their staff and surfers to get more involved in the projects they are funding and support.

Philanthropy has now become another important element for some professional surfers. Rob Machado, who was interviewed by Ponting in a video presentation, carries out his philanthropic work in San Diego County through the Rob Machado Foundation. The iconic Cardiff surfer also worked with Reef to create a more sustainable sandal made from recycled tires.

One of the better-received presentations was by Kevin Whilden, cofounder of Sustainable Surf, who identifies and implements environmental solutions for the surf industry. The start-up organization has helped to collect thousands of pounds of used Styrofoam that is then collected, compressed, and reused in recycled expanded polystyrene surfboard blanks.

These blanks produced by Marko Foam only cost five dollars more than those that are non-recycled, and according to Whilden, "are ten percent stronger." Sustainable Surf partnered with Rip

Curl and Wastebusters at the San Francisco Rip Curl Pro to reduce waste by ninety percent.

It is solutions like these and green and social entrepreneurs such as Whilden, Aabo, and the new plethora of members of surfing's new "aloha" generation who are changing what has typically been a group of inward-looking athletes into a community that is paying more attention to philanthropy.

Jake Stutz, a High Tech High School sophomore who attended the forum, exemplifies this new generation. Recently returned from a school trip to Nicaragua, Jake and his classmates volunteered for community development projects and surfed great waves. "It was cool," he said.

Chapter 8
THE BEST WORST BEACH MOVIES

For my generation, summer evenings were often spent at the local drive-in watching whatever blockbuster or B movie that happened to be on the marquee. If we were lucky, we might have caught a masterpiece like *The Godfather Part II* or *Jaws*, the best summer beach movie of all time. More than likely the marquee listed B movies and cult favorites such as *Women in Cages*, *Malibu Beach*, *Foxy Brown*, and *Macon County Line*.

Starting in 1959 with the release of *Gidget*, starring Sandra Dee and La Jolla's Cliff Robertson, the summer beach movie has been a Hollywood B movie staple. Unfortunately, *Gidget* was a high-water mark for the '60s-era beach surf flicks that soon became exemplified by the Frankie Avalon and Annette Funicello *Beach Party* films that made surfers look like the idiots everyone thinks we are.

Love them or hate them, beach flicks are an important part of the pop culture landscape and defined Southern California in the minds of many Americans. Here are some of the best worst beach movies.

1. *Roller Boogie* (1979)

Hands down, *Roller Boogie* is the best worst beach picture of all time. Who could have imagined that at the same time Tony Alva and his gang were in the midst of the gritty skateboard explosion in Venice Beach, aka Dogtown, legions of gay roller skaters were cruising the boardwalk in spandex short shorts and rainbow suspenders.

Dude, this is the funniest, campiest beach exploitation film ever! Linda Blair is so bad, the plot so preposterous, that *Roller Boogie* actually works as a contemporary Will Ferrell-style '70s exploitation film remake.

The hero, played by real roller skating champion Jim Bray, dreams of becoming an Olympic gold medalist in roller dancing! He is championed by Linda Blair (who can't act), and at some point the plot goes Andy Hardy but with a skate competition instead of a dance. A crooked developer and his goons are thrown in toward the end to give the film some social redemption.

There is even a chubby beach beat cop who channels the Village People's Victor Willis in short-shorts and a tight white T-shirt. The best part is the chase scene on roller skates in which the good guys (the skaters) pelt the bad buys with fruit (wink-wink) and then skate through a skateboard park that is only inhabited by the already-mentioned spandex-wearing roller skaters.

The best part of the *Roller Boogie* experience was watching it with my thirteen-year-old son, who laughed in amazement along with me. So parents, feel free to boost your core score by watching *Roller Boogie* with your teens. And since this disaster is filled with buxom, Farrah-haired, roller-boogie hotties in French-cut bikinis, my son asked, "Dad, were all the girls like that in the seventies?"

2. In God's Hands (1998)

Arguably one of the worst movies ever made. I'm not even sure what the plot is supposed to be about. More than likely the screenplay consisted of endless pages of undecipherable scribbles. Ironically, sexploitation director Zalman King made this straight so Matt George and Shane Dorian spend the movie mumbling incoherently as they traipse around the tropics. Apparently the movie is supposed to be about something meaningful, but only in a faux Euro-serious way. Even the surfing sucks.

3. *Beach Blanket Bingo* and all the Frankie Avalon and Annette Funicello movies (1960s)

This is what you'd get if a retro version of *Jersey Shore* was reimagined as *Laguna Beach*, but with dancing and dumber stars. That pretty much sums up all the Beach Party movies of the mid-'60s. All of these flicks are terrible enough to qualify as essential cult favorites. The only problem is that you have to be really drunk to enjoy watching them.

4. *The Van* (1977)

This low-budget, lackluster B movie could have been one of the great teen exploitation films of all time, but the forgettable cast (except for Danny DeVito) killed its chances. The plot goes something like this: a bro named Bobby graduates from high school, spends the summer cruising for chicks, and working at a car wash (apparently this was the last time in history that car washes weren't staffed by ex-cons). He saves enough money to buy a killer custom van, a '70s dream machine complete with a waterbed and shag carpeting.

Bobby can't get the stuck-up valedictorian to like him, but after scoring with beach babes, he and the smart chick hit it off. They cruise a custom van gathering at an LA County beach parking lot where they meet all kinds of groovy '70s van people, including the obligatory black guys in fedora hats, and fall in love. You couldn't make this stuff up, so sit through *The Van* because you'll laugh for all the right reasons.

5. *Point Break* **(1991)**

This action flick should have been the best surfing movie ever made. Directed by up-and-coming action director Kathryn Bigelow (who went on to win an Academy Award for *The Hurt Locker*), and with Patrick Swayze as Bodhi and Keanu Reeves as Johnny Utah, with stand-in surfing by Dino Andino, it was the film that made us all embarrassed to be surfers.

With a story set in Huntington Beach that echoes some of the scenes in Kem Nunn's novel *Tapping the Source*, Reeves plays an undercover cop whose boss, Gary Busey (before he was sideswiped on his motorcycle and suffered permanent foggy brain), figures out that a string of bank robberies must be perpetuated by surfers since the robbers have tan lines.

Although the action set pieces are truly spectacular (Bigelow is an action genius), the dialogue is wooden and everyone is either a drug dealer, machine-gun salesman, or bikini model-philosopher. Oh, and the surf always seems to be blown out and everyone surfs mostly at night. Even through a remake will be released in the summer of 2015 with Venezuelan anti-hero Edgar Ramirez as Bodhi and Australian Luke Bracey as Johnny Utah, nothing could ever top the original's total awesomeness.

Chapter 9

BEACH MOVIES WE HATE TO LOVE

One cure for the midwinter blues (besides facing the fact that winter is the best time to hit the beach) is to make some popcorn, curl up on the couch, and check out one of these ultra fun beach movies.

1. *Fast Times at Ridgemont High*

Face it, Sean Penn as Jeff Spicoli, a semisavant, airhead lamebrain is the best film portrayal of a surfer ever (with the exception of Jay Adams as himself in *Dogtown and Z-Boys*.) Directed by Amy Heckerling (who went on to even better stuff in *Clueless*) and penned by San Diego's own Cameron Crowe, *Fast Times* nails late 70s / early 80s Southern California teen culture, before John Hughes moved the nexus of teen lollapalooza to the Midwest with movies like *The Breakfast Club* and *Ferris Bueller's Day Off*.

The best thing about *Fast Times* is its crazy good cast, including Judge Reinhold, Phoebe Cates (so babelicious!), Forest Whitaker, Eric Stolz (who Quentin Tarantino would later allow to update his role as a drug dealer in *Pulp Fiction*), Anthony Edwards, Nicolas Cage, rocker goddess Nancy Wilson (who Crowe later married), and Ray Walston as Mr. Hand, the high school teacher we all remember hating. With lots of nudity, sex, drinking, and drugs, you probably don't want your teens to watch this, but more than likely they already have.

2. Valley Girl (1983)

Nicolas Cage wins over valley-beach princess Julie, played by Deborah Foreman, in this underrated '80s teen flick. With lots of screen time for LA power pop indie gods the Plimsouls, in *Valley Girl*—like in all great teen pics—the key romancing takes place at the beach. Cage updates the stereotypical "greaser" role into that of a Hollywood punker and woos his dream girl on the sands of Santa Monica.

Valley Girl was helmed by Martha Coolidge, who went on to discover and direct Val Kilmer in the '80s classic *Real Genius*. *Valley Girl* is a companion piece to Moon Zappa's horrible and ultra ironic "Valley Girl," arguably the best-worst white girl rap song ever.

3. Malibu Beach (1978) /*Van Nuys Blvd.* (1979)

The best thing about this absolutely lame but lovable twofer from the exploitation kings at Crown International Pictures was the appearance of James Daughton as Bobby in *Malibu Beach*. Daughton later went on to fame as fascist frat boy Greg Marmalard in *Animal House* (the best college movie ever). These no-plot teen flicks were drive-in staples during the late '70s (I caught them at the now-defunct Palm Theater in Imperial Beach) and feature characters such as Dugie (a Speedo-wearing, greased-up bodybuilder) and Chooch (a porn-mustached, hot rod racer) who channels Harrison Ford's Bob Falfa from *American Graffiti* while ripping off Henry Winkler's Fonz.

Malibu Beach features an endless parade of airhead bimbos and bros driving the oak-lined streets of Malibu while drunk or stoned on their way to the beach to have sex. The likewise plotless *Van Nuys Blvd.*, a sub-grade rip-off of George Lucas's *American Graffiti*, features even dumber teens who cruise around in custom vans while drunk or stoned on their way to have sex at the drive-up burger shack (which is like, totally awesome). The best thing about these films is that Richard Linklater used them as templates for his super cool *Dazed and Confused*, which is the best teen film of all time. For some reason, both *Malibu Beach* and *Van Nuys Blvd.* appeared on Netflix streaming and then disappeared. Hopefully you can catch them again very, very soon.

4. *The Sure Thing* (1985)

The film that introduced us to the awkward John Cusack that we came to know and love in *Say Anything, Grosse Pointe Blank* and *High Fidelity,* this romantic flick directed by Rob Reiner is a gem. Cusack teamed up with Daphne Zuniga (*Melrose Place*) and super dude Anthony Edwards on this road trip to Malibu along with the "Sure Thing," played by ultra hottie Nicollette Sheridan. This is a homage (sort of) to Frank Capra's Oscar-winning *It Happened One Night,* although with no redeeming social value, except for the fact that it is still really, really charming.

5. *Weekend at Bernie's* (1989)

An annoying but fun teen exploitation flick starring Jonathan Silverman and Andrew McCarthy a few years after he wooed Molly Ringwald in *Pretty in Pink* and decades before he morphed into a perceptive travel writer. *Weekend* takes place at an East Coast beach mansion, which explains why all the bad guys are all neon-suit-wearing mobsters with bad haircuts. Terry Kiser plays Bernie, the dead guy, who at one point is taken water-skiing by McCarthy and Silverman while he's dead. This is one of the those films that doesn't stand the test of time, but with characters named Paulie, Vito, Tina, and Tawny, how can you resist? Plus, your kids will love it.

Other honorable mentions include the lovable *Lifeguard* (Sam Elliott as cool as ever), *Mamma Mia!,* and *Blue Hawaii. The Beach* isn't that fun and *Cast Away* is long and kind of a drag. *Some Like It Hot* didn't make my list because this classic and brilliant Billy Wilder comedy (as in one of the best, ever) starring Tony Curtis and Marilyn Monroe—that was filmed in Coronado—will forever be a beach picture that we love to love.

Chapter 10
THE BEST OCEAN FILMS OF ALL TIME

There is something about ocean films that bring me back to my childhood. Maybe it was my love for Robert Louis Stevenson's *Treasure Island* or being mesmerized by Jules Verne's *20,000 Leagues Under the Sea*. Add the wonderful memories of watching *The Undersea World of Jacques Cousteau* on television with my family, and I'm a sucker for anything to do with the sea. Here are my candidates for the best ocean films of all time.

1. *The Life Aquatic with Steve Zissou* (2004)

A highly eccentric and original homage to Jacques Cousteau with a little bit of Fellini thrown in, *The Life Aquatic* features Bill Murray as washed up ocean explorer Steve Zissou, who searches for the elusive Jaguar shark to revive his career and avenge the death of his longtime friend and partner Esteban. The film also stars Owen Wilson, Cate Blanchett, Anjelica Huston, Willem Dafoe, Jeff Goldblum, and cult favorite Bud Cort. The crew partakes in an underwater odyssey and madcap adventures on Zissou's research vessel *The Belafonte*. In *The Life Aquatic*, director-producer Wes Anderson creates a funny and unique film that is a love letter to our romance with the sea. Mark Mothersbaugh, formerly of Devo, provides the ultra cool soundtrack.

2. *Jaws* (1975)

With *Jaws*, director Steven Spielberg launched Hollywood into an obsession with action-packed, high-concept blockbusters and furthered the legend of the great white shark. While the mechanical shark doesn't hold up, who could ever forget the dazzling brilliance of Robert Shaw as the maniacal sea dog Quint. The suspenseful scene in which Shaw tells the tale of being surrounded by sharks after surviving the sinking of the USS *Indianapolis* during World War II—while Roy Scheider and Richard Dreyfuss listen on and the shark silently closes in—is still riveting. Based on Peter Benchley's bestselling book of the same name, *Jaws* destroyed any opportunity to educate the public about the critical role that sharks play in maintaining the health of ocean ecosystems and made the ocean a scary place for people who don't know better.

3. *The Cove* (2009)

The Cove is *Ocean's Eleven* meets *Flipper* and an action-packed, Oscar-winning, emotionally charged caper film. Director Louie Psihoyos tells the tale of dolphin trainer turned ocean activist Ric O'Barry as he tries to uncover and stop the brutal and unnecessary slaughter of dolphins in Taiji, Japan. Unfortunately, the massacres in Taiji continue, but Psihoyos and O'Barry show why the world needs ocean conservationists.

4. *Master and Commander: The Far Side of the World* (2003)

In *Master and Commander*, Australian director Peter Weir does a brilliant job of translating Patrick O'Brian's Jack Aubrey series of books into a wonderfully romantic and epic ocean film that deservedly received an Oscar for Best Cinematography. Russell Crowe stars as Captain "Lucky Jack" Aubrey who commands the HMS *Surprise* to pursue the French privateer *Acheron* around the New World. The scenes of exploration in the Galápagos Islands are breathtaking, and the depiction of field surgery and the travails of transoceanic sailing remind us of how lucky we are to live in the modern age. This is an intelligent and beautifully made film suitable for the entire family.

5. *Mutiny on the Bounty* (1935)

Has there ever been an actor more magnetic than Clark Gable as Fletcher Christian and a villain so unlikable as Charles Laughton's William Bligh? Laughton's depiction as Bligh is a precursor to Darth Vader—a flawed and evil servant of the empire. This Oscar winner for Best Picture tells the story of the HMS *Bounty*'s two-year voyage to Tahiti in 1787. The 1935 version of *Mutiny of the Bounty* is a romantic and classic example of old-school Hollywood at its best.

Other notable ocean films include: *Titanic, The Abyss, Das Boot, The Hunt for Red October, The Big Blue, The Little Mermaid, Pirates of the Caribbean, 20,000 Leagues Under the Sea, Wind, The Secret of Roan Inish, White Squall,* and *Captains Courageous.*

Chapter 11
THE BEST SURF FILMS OF ALL TIME

Most surf movies are incredibly boring surf "porn," with repeated barrels, aerial maneuvers, tropical locales, and hipster soundtracks. They are perfect for groms and TV screens at beach eateries and bars, but fail to meet basic cinematic storytelling standards.

Luckily, a few filmmakers have done their best to introduce audiences to the themes that make surfing a unique sport. These directors, Bruce Brown, Stacy Peralta, John Milius, and Jeremy Gosch all made great films first and surfing films second. The best surf films touch on themes rarely examined by everyday surfers and involve some of the sport's brightest stars, writers, and most iconoclastic and idiosyncratic surfers.

1. *The Endless Summer* (1966)

In the early 1960s, pioneer surf filmmaker Bruce Brown set off on a trip around the world with Mike Hynson and Robert August, two young surfers from Southern California, on a quest for an "endless" summer. They scored waves in Senegal, roamed across apartheid-era South Africa, rode endless peelers at Cape St. Francis, and surfed backwash in Tahiti.

The sense of humor and sympathetic and silent performances of Hynson and August, combined with the deadpan narration of

Brown, made this a national hit in 1966. *Endless Summer* has defined surf travel for generations, and still holds up as a timeless narrative on the innocence of surfing and the friendship that still link surfing and surfers around the globe. If you haven't yet embarked on your own *Endless Summer*, free of surf camps and a calendar, then watch the film and live your dream.

2. *Dogtown and Z-Boys* (2001)

A decade after clean-cut Hynson and August traipsed around the world in mod suits and Ray-Bans, a collection of scruffy kids from the wrong side of the tracks in Santa Monica and Venice— or Dogtown—took the radical Hawaiian vertical surfing style epitomized by Larry Bertlemann, Buttons Kaluhiokalani, and Mark Liddell and applied it to the waves of Venice, as well as the streets, banks, and pools of Southern California.

Dogtown and Z-Boys is Stacy Peralta's brilliant homage to his youth in which he dug deep and came up with a stunning deconstruction of Southern California surf and skate culture. Brilliantly written and directed, everything is pitch-perfect in this documentary that sheds light on 1970s-era surf and skate scene that until recently was a lost decade. The fictional version, *The Lords of Dogtown*, was filmed in Imperial Beach and is an admirable attempt to convey the era, but falls way short of Peralta's documentary.

3. *Big Wednesday* (1978)

I still remember watching this John Milius-directed film at the Vogue Theater in Chula Vista when it first came out. My buddies and I laughed at all the right moments, were in awe of the surfing finale, loved the stylish surfing, and understood the changing of the guard storyline.

Cowriters Milius and Denny Aaberg were Malibu surfers who in *Big Wednesday* managed to capture the end of the longboard era, Vietnam, big-wave surfing, the beginning of surfing professionalism, and the essence of surfing and style. Originally written off by surfers and critics, *Big Wednesday* ultimately earned the respect it deserves. The classic dialogue (Milius was a screenwriting genius, responsible for *Apocalypse Now* and classic lines in *Dirty Harry*), fight scenes, Gary Busey's Leroy "The Masochist" combing his hair with a fish, the Tijuana trip, the epic draft registration set piece, and stylish surfing all make this a fun and required family surf movie.

The surfing and cinematography in *Big Wednesday* are top-notch. Water stunt doubles included Peter "PT" Townend, Bill Hamilton, Bruce Raymond, Jackie Dunn, J. Riddle, Ian Cairns, and Gerry Lopez playing himself. Legendary cameramen Dan Merkel, Bud Browne, Greg MacGillivray, and George Greenough did an outstanding job capturing the surfing and beautiful waves on film, especially the finale at Sunset Beach. *Big Wednesday* is the *Casablanca* of surf films: timeless, beautifully conceived and executed classic American cinema.

4. *Bustin' Down the Door* (2009)

In the early to mid '70s, a small group of feral and extremely talented Australian and South African surfers such as Shaun Tomson, Mark Richards, Ian Cairns, Michael Tomson, Peter Townend, and Wayne "Rabbit" Bartholomew assembled each winter on Oahu's North Shore to surf the best waves and become the world's best surfers. In the process they invented professional surfing and disrespected Hawaiian culture. This brilliant and moving film unflinchingly tells that story with no holds barred. With the help of an insightful and contemplative Barry "BK" Kanaiaupuni, who with Jeff Hakman is the lead storyteller on the Hawaiian side, *Bustin' Down the Door* tells the compelling and emotional tale of how surfing's professional pioneers became victims of their own hubris and end up finding their own humility and humanity.

Bustin' Down the Door is great and essential filmmaking. Surfers are generally unable to examine themselves honestly, but watching Rabbit discuss his childhood poverty is moving. As a grom in the '70s, all these guys were my heroes and their surfing still holds up for its beauty, radicalism, originality, and precision.

5. *Riding Giants* (2004)

Riding Giants, Bustin' Down the Door, and *Dogtown* are about as close to the definitive historical and social texts on surfing as you'll find. In *Riding Giants*, Stacy Peralta shows what it is like to be in a wild ocean and illuminates the surfing lives and psyches of Greg Noll, Laird Hamilton, Maverick's pioneer Jeff Clark, and Hamilton's tow partner Dave Kalama (a great surfer in his own right).

The footage is incredible; the personalities, stories, and histories are compelling; and the film once again benefits from Peralta's expert direction and production values. If you can read William Finnegan's brilliant "Playing Doc's Games" from the *New Yorker*, after you view *Riding Giants* and *Bustin' Down the Door*, then you've hit the surfing trifecta.

Chapter 12
WHY I HATE LOCALISM

I n the middle of the night—August 26, 1942—a group of French police under the orders of the Nazis rounded up a group of Jewish families in Nice. My father's family, including his aunt Anna and cousins Bernard and Lisette, were among those taken to military barracks. There, according to Bernard's widow, Dorothy Fall, in her book *Bernard Fall: Memoirs of a Soldier-Scholar*, "They all mingled in the filth and heat for a week."

My great-uncle Leo, husband to Anna and father of Bernard and Lisette, was later tortured and murdered by the Gestapo in November 1943 while he lay sick in a hospital bed.

The effort of the Nazis to exclude Jews and other groups of people from everyday life in Europe (and then exterminate them) was the ultimate form of localism. Longtime residents and citizens of France, including my own father, were delisted as "locals" or residents and all their rights—and in many cases, their lives—were forfeited.

As a young surfer in the late 1970s and early 1980s in Southern California, I witnessed bullying, intimidation, and violence in the water and on the beach. Gangs of self-described surfing "locals" used violence and intimidation to prevent "non-locals" from using public space. In some cases localism was ignored and/or abetted by the local police.

Southern California has a long history of excluding "non-locals" from beaches. Until recently, some residents of Malibu contracted private guards to illegally keep the public from using public beaches. In the 1920s, Bruce's Beach in Manhattan Beach was the only beach in all of Los Angeles County open to people of all races.

Unfortunately, groups of thugs or self-described "locals" still populate the coastline and harass anyone they deem to be a "non-local." They often use violence to prevent surfers from using public space. Localism reflects "the increasing ecology of privatization and socio-economic segmentation in American cities," said Larry Herzog, professor of urban planning at San Diego State University. "We have become a nation of gated communities, and the 'ecology of fear.' Surfers, without realizing it, are channeling a preference for personal space, fenced yards or marked territory, and the unfamiliarity with being 'public,' or gracious about sharing a public space, like the ocean."

I asked Kevin Keenan, director of the San Diego branch of the ACLU, if the act of harassing or intimidating anyone from using public space, in this case the coast and ocean, violates fundamental American civil liberties. "In *US v. Allen*, the 9th Circuit," Keenan wrote, "held that a band of racist thugs who patrolled a public park and kicked out some people through threats and intimidation based on their race were violating their federal civil rights (a federal crime).

"You could argue that civil rights law protects against chasing people off a beach or wave based on their race, color, religion, or national origin, but should also extend to other kinds of groups, like where a person resides," said Keenan. "Not incidentally, given segregation in our society and other reasons, where a person resides often relates closely to race, color, religion, and national origin."

The sad fact is that most surfers don't practice localism, but most do little if anything to prevent it. Engaging in localism is different than regulating a lineup. That can be done quietly and requires the type of leadership skills that hothead angry "locals" don't have.

I wish being a local meant being invested in the conservation and stewardship of a surf spot. Imagine a world in which surfers worked together to save surfing areas instead of screaming and fighting with each other over who has the right to rule the lineup. We would catch more waves, be happier, and have a greater number of spots to surf.

Chapter 13

HOW SURFERS CAN SAVE GAS AND SAVE THE PLANET

With gas prices at record levels, commuters, and especially surfers, are scrambling to reduce their fuel consumption. Surfers often waste gas while driving nonstop coastal loops in search of the best waves, and let their vehicle idle endlessly during street-end or beach parking lot surf checks.

Surfers love their gas guzzling, bro-dude, monster surf mobiles that boost macho core-scores, but put a strain on bank accounts and produce smog alerts. A fair share of surfers pack their quiver in the back of a lifted 4x4 with giant tires, which makes sense when hauling a trailer filled with sand toys to the desert, but not so much when driving a mile to the beach.

There are, however, some creative and innovative ways to save fuel, the planet, and money in order to spend the day at the beach. Although for some conservatives, "conservation" is a dirty word, for this old-school cheapo, anything that directs less of my paycheck to the monolithic retrograde oil industry and all the dictators who love to sell us petroleum, is a good thing.

Trade In Your Gas Guzzler

For everyone who bought their mega-truck on zero percent

financing and now pays one hundred and twenty dollars to fill the gas tank, run to your nearest auto dealer and trade it in for a hybrid or electric vehicle. My hybrid averages about forty MPG and fits four groms besides me. With the money I save on gas, I can afford to buy my kids and their friends tacos at Rubio's after a run to Black's. If your kids don't like your new wheels with less legroom, make them hitchhike.

Carpool

You know that really mean and grumpy silverback that screams at you everyday in the lineup even though you've surfed together for more than twenty years and live down the street from him? Well, next time he lovingly blasts you with an insult, pitch him on a carpool.

As in, "Hey bro—look, I know surfing makes you incomprehensibly angry, but why don't I ease your pain by joining you on the beach commute and we'll share some tasty waves together?"

Paint a picture of all the fun you'll have and even offer to let him slap you around in front of his crew for spilling yerba maté on his ride. So make some new friends, save some money, and bring peace and joy to your spot by bringing carpooling to your lineup.

Recover a Bike from the Trash and Ride It to the Beach

I come from a long line of hardened Dumpster divers, or what eco-hipsters now call "freegans." As a kid I roamed the streets salvaging bikes, surfboards, wet suits, and anything else that could propel me to the beach and in the water. I still continue that tradition with my kids and often depend on the largesse of my eighty-year-old immigrant father, who is the Freegan King of California. We have a bevy of old bicycles we've cobbled together as urban surf machines. The bicycles my kids learned on came from a Dumpster run. We fixed them up together.

I'm currently cruising an '80s Schwinn ten-speed girl's beach cruiser that my father liberated from the trash. I've outfitted it with

Carver surf racks and a big basket. No more parking problems, and I burn a few more calories during my daily surf commute.

With gas above four dollars a gallon, more people are switching to bike surf commutes. So search the streets and alleys of your local millionaire-laden beach town (La Jolla is gold) and enjoy the gifts of our throwaway consumer society in order to save money, get in shape, and improve air quality.

Take the Bus

The Southern California coastal region is filled with trains and buses. A monthly pass costs anywhere from seventy-two dollars for adults to eighteen dollars for seniors. So go ahead and make a few friends while swinging your longboard around the bus during the morning beach commute. Last year my kids and their friend Jake caught the ferry, two buses, and the Coaster from Imperial Beach to San Clemente in order to spend a few days surfing Lowers, and it only took five hours one way. Time is money and since no one seems to have any money, spend your time wisely, meet new people, and cruise to the waves in our wonderful transit system.

Stop Surfing

Your significant other and Mom are correct—-surfing in an incredibly selfish and self-centered activity that accomplishes very little and interferes with your job, life, and relationships. So nix surfing, reduce your overhead, and spend more time at home with your spouse and children. Who knows, they might even remember who you are.

Chapter 14

HURRICANE SANDY AND SAND REPLENISHMENT

As I watched the news reports of the devastation caused by Hurricane Sandy's storm surge, I wondered what would happen to Southern California if a similar storm hit. Imperial Beach, where I live, is a low-lying coastal city that borders the ocean, the southern end of San Diego Bay, and the Tijuana Estuary. Any storm with a potent tidal surge could easily flood the homes, dunes, and streets of my hometown.

Understanding the impact of Sandy on the beaches, barrier islands, and cities of the East Coast is critical for the residents of Southern California in order to evaluate the costly efforts to preserve local beaches. Now that the San Diego Association of Governments (SANDAG) completed a $28 million regional sand replenishment project throughout San Diego County coastal areas, we need to ask if having government agencies continue to spend billions of dollars nationally dumping sand on our beaches to forestall their inevitable reduction in size due to man-made erosion, violent storms, and sea level rise is really worth it. That is especially true in light of new proposals by the Army Corps of Engineers to spend $261 million on sand projects just for Encinitas, Solana Beach, and San Clemente.

"Beach replenishment and beach nourishment are euphemisms for what are really beach dredge and fill that turns the beach into an industrial site during construction," said Surfrider Foundation Executive Director Chad Nelsen. "They should be designed to minimize impacts to nearshore reefs that are important recreational and ecological resources."

Terry Gibson, a longtime surfer and fisherman from Florida, has spent a considerable amount of effort evaluating the impacts of badly managed sand replenishment projects on the East Coast. "Nearshore reefs or other types of essential fish habitat are typically buried or silted over, without adequate much less kind-for-kind mitigation," said Gibson. "Chronic turbidity is often a problem. The entire slope of the nearshore environment typically changes so that wave quality from a surfer's perspective is degraded or destroyed. And you often lose the qualities that make a beach attractive to sea turtles, not to mention the impacts to the invertebrates that live in the beach and are a requisite forage source for fish and birds."

The San Diego chapter of the Surfrider Foundation is monitoring the impacts to surf throughout San Diego from the current SANDAG regional effort via video monitoring. In Imperial Beach the SANDAG project has shut down the surf for about seventy-five percent of our beachfront.

"At Imperial Beach we've been seeing a trend toward decreasing surfer counts and decreasing ride length," said Tom Cook, a researcher at the Scripps Institution of Oceanography.

These giant sand projects are relics of the past that do not reflect our climate-contorted and fiscally prudent future.

As of October 2014, the SANDAG sand project in Imperial Beach has significantly impacted surf quality, exacerbated coastal flooding for some coastal residents, and may have increased impacts to public infrastructure. Additionally, a large quantity of the sand moved south of the project area into the Tijuana River Mouth State Marine Conservation Area and Tijuana Slough National Wildlife Refuge shorelines.

Chapter 15

WHY THE CALIFORNIA COASTAL ACT MATTERS

In 1971, I accompanied my mother and little brother, Nicky, to sand dunes on the shore of San Diego Bay at the southern edge of the Silver Strand in Coronado. I still remember the fear I felt when a security guard with a gun approached us.

"This is private property and you are trespassing," the guard told us (the area was later developed as the Coronado Cays).

"How dare that man scare us with his gun," said my mother.

That incident occurred before California voters approved the passage of the Coastal Act in 1976.

"I never take for granted California's stunning coast, or the foresight of those who passed the Coastal Act four decades ago to keep it accessible to people all over the state," said Karen Garrison of the Natural Resources Defense Council.

The problem with the Coastal Commission is that the agency "can set the rules, but it can't enforce them," said Chad Nelsen of the Surfrider Foundation. "Imagine what the roads would be like if the police couldn't issue traffic tickets. That is essentially the plight of the Coastal Commission with regard to beach access."

Ten years ago, Wallace J. Nichols trekked twelve hundred miles from Oregon to Mexico along the coastal trail. "I witnessed firsthand the diversity of people who love the ocean and I saw how some people, particularly around LA, were fighting to keep it for themselves, despite clear laws protecting the coast and providing public access for all," he said.

For Warner Chabot, "The Coastal Act initiative was the result of public outrage over landowners blocking access to the coast. Now there are more than 1,944 Coast Act violations of which 690 are in Los Angeles County and of those 533 are in Malibu, and 123 are in San Diego."

To remedy this situation, San Diego Assembly Member Toni Atkins introduced AB 976, which gives the California Coastal Commission the ability to levy limited fines for Coastal Act violations. A similar enforcement tool is already in place for twenty-one other state regulatory agencies, including the State Water Resources Control Board, the Air Resources Board, and the State Lands Commission.

"Free and open coastal access is critical to the health and well-being of our communities," said Ben McCue of Outdoor Outreach, an organization that takes kids from low-income communities on outings to the beach.

Making sure everyone can use the beach will require agencies to enforce the laws voters passed. We should ensure that private property owners cannot continue to obstruct the natural and legal rights of the public to enjoy resources that belong to us all.

After all, "A day at the beach is a right all Californians are entitled to enjoy," said Marce Gutierrez of Azul.

———

The California Coastal Commission now has the authority to fine homeowners for violating the Coastal Act, especially when they attempt to block public access to the coast.

Chapter 16

CLIMATE CHANGE IN SOUTHERN CALIFORNIA

With ongoing Hurricane Sandy cleanup operations and damage assessment being carried out on the Eastern Seaboard, it is easy for Californians to become complacent and argue that climate change cannot happen here. For surfers, however, subtle but significant changes in our climate have already had a big impact on our coastline and even surfing conditions.

The dramatic oscillations in ocean temperatures, changes in weather patterns, increased Santa Ana conditions, and increasing loss of coastline due to erosion are all things long-term surfers and ocean observers already see happening. As a drought-prone region largely dependent on water from the Sierra Nevada and the Colorado River, we are vulnerable to increases in temperatures, prolonged drought, and sea level rise.

Dangerous wildfires experienced in the past decade may be indicative of what the residents of California and elsewhere can expect in the future. The issue is not whether or not California is being impacted by climate change. Our climate is already changing. The fundamental issue that we need to address is how we as a state will adapt and respond to our changing climate.

We can bury our head in the sand and pretend that climate change is a hoax. Or we can believe the streams of data assessed by climate scientists worldwide to understand that we have an obligation to identify solutions that can help deal with the changes that are happening now and forecast to come—before it is too late.

The time to deal with climate change in California is right now. In San Diego, for example, the San Diego Foundation has provided a blueprint, *San Diego's Changing Climate: A Regional Wake-Up Call* (note my wife, Emily Young, helped prepare and write the report) to identify some of the ways in which our climate is changing now and is forecast to change.

The report evaluates how San Diego's climate will change by 2050 if current trends continue. Some of the impacts of climate change in San Diego County listed in the foundation's report include:

- We will see an increase in average annual temperatures of between 1.5–4.5 degrees.

- The weather in November will often feel like September does.

- Summers will be even hotter than they are now.

- There is projected to be an increase in sea level between 12–18 inches, exacerbating the loss of beaches.

- We will need thirty-seven percent more water than we currently utilize even though our sources of water might shrink by twenty percent.

- There will be an increase by twenty percent of the number of days with ideal conditions for large fires.

It is not too late to take action. I sat on the City of Chula Vista Climate Change Working Group and was impressed by how business leaders, conservationists, and scientists came together to adopt a number of common sense and low-cost strategies to reduce the impact of climate change (just planting more trees would help). Planning for climate change and sea level rise is something that every city in California should undertake. We cannot afford not to.

Chapter 17

SAVING WAVES AT THE GLOBAL WAVE CONFERENCE

"We are more than a wave," said Pablo Narvaez of Barra de la Cruz. Considered one of the world's best waves by *Surfer* magazine, Barra is also an indigenous coastal village in Mexico where surfing is the main source of tourist revenues. "We have sea turtles, a mangrove lagoon, and a beautiful village filled with culture," said Pablo.

Pablo was among surf conservationists from nineteen organizations representing ten countries who came together in Rosarito Beach at the 3rd Global Wave Conference (GWC), the world's largest gathering dedicated to global wave protection. The conference was held to discuss experiences and strategies to protect coastal ecosystems and resources.

"Over the last decade the surf conservation movement has blossomed but until recently the world's surf protection groups have been working in isolation," said, Surfrider Executive Director Chad Nelsen. "The Global Wave Conference is designed to change that and promote exchange of knowledge and programs, information sharing and collaboration, with the larger goal to establish a unified front for global wave protection."

The conference represents a growing understanding that the world's coastlines, and more specifically its surf spots, are important economical, ecological, cultural, and recreational resources that must be protected.

"The GWC was a really productive and amazing conference, from local fishermen in Baja, to nonprofit leaders in the UK, to representatives from the UNDP in Costa Rica. The true strength of the conference was to create new and innovative partnerships among all surf users," said Save the Waves Executive Director Nik Strong-Cvetich.

In Rosarito Beach, a number of the attendees represented communities from Mexico and Latin America who are striving to conserve their waves, beaches, and ways of life through surfing tourism and conservation.

"Representation from small coastal fishing and surfing villages put a spotlight on some great examples of surf protection taking place under the radar in Mexico, one of the most popular countries for surf tourism on the globe," said Zach Plopper, who works with me at WILDCOAST.

Conference participants discussed strategies to protect coastal access and surf spots. Fernando Marvan from Surf Ens presented on the proposed Bahia Todos Santos World Surfing Reserve. Carlos Luna of Rosarito Beach and Alfredo Ramirez of UAPO discussed youth surfing in the region and the future of the sport in Baja California. "Waves are natural resources. It is up to us to protect them. As ocean lovers we need to spread the love and also educate young surfers about our environment," said Alfredo, who organizes youth surfing contests and lessons in both the US and Mexico. "They are the next generation that will take care of our coasts."

Artemio Murillo and Jaime Villavicencio traveled all of the way from the fishing village of Bahia Asuncion in Baja California Sur to make a presentation on how surfing has been a catalyst for coastal stewardship. Jaime fixes up old surfboards in his remote village so that local kids can surf.

One of the most impressive talks was by Narvaez, who discussed how his Oaxaca town of eight hundred people is able to conserve its coast. "We charge a fee to use our beach services. Those monies in turn fund community projects and medical care for every member of our village," said Pablo.

Representatives from Surfers Against Sewage (UK), Save the Waves (US), Salvem o Surf (Portugal), Surfrider Europe (France), Surfers' Environmental Alliance (US), Canary Island Surfing Federation, Desarrollo y Gestión Costera (Peru), and the Osa and Golfito Initiative (Costa Rica) all gave presentations. "Every wave is unique. Every beach is important for the community," said Carlo Grigoletto, the executive director of Desarrollo y Gestión Costera.

The conference concluded with a field trip to Ensenada to view some of the efforts being carried out by local NGOs and the proposed location of Mexico's first world surfing reserve in Bahia Todos Santos.

As an act of solidarity, the groups attending the Global Wave Conference agreed to support Surfers Against Sewage's Protect Our Waves campaign, which is designed to increase legal protection for surfing in the UK. "It was great to see the commitment, tenacity and innovative approaches surfers are using to protect the waves they love all over the planet," said former Surfrider Foundation Executive Director Jim Moriarty.

PART III

Travel

 Steve McQueen and I rode our motorcycles down to Cabo back before the road was paved. We'd stay at these little ranchos each night. When we got to Cabo, which was basically nothing, we found a cargo plane, road our bikes up it, and flew back to LA.

—Bruce Brown

Chapter 18

A PILGRIMAGE TO BELLS

Most surfers who travel to Australia tour the world-class surf spots of northern New South Wales and Southern Queensland (the Gold Coast). But on a sabbatical trip to Australia in the summer of 2009, Israel, Daniel, and I traveled through the less populated surf coast of southern New South Wales and Victoria, described in our *Surfing Australia* guidebook as "a surf explorer's dream."

The first part of our trip was to be a six-week pilgrimage south from Sydney along the coastal Princes Highway to Bells Beach. Then Emily would join us, and we would spend another week in Australia and three weeks in New Zealand.

The boys and I arrived at Sydney Airport in the early morning after a long flight from San Diego. We hailed a taxi van and hauled our five surfboards and canvas duffel bags filled with camping and surfing gear to the Kea Campervan rental center on the outskirts of Sydney. There we picked up a 2006 VW diesel pop-top camper van that was to be our home for the next seven weeks.

South of Sydney, the Princes Highway skirts the forest of Royal National Park, the world's second-oldest national park, and then descends onto the coast at the village of Stanwell Park. Our first view of the beach was what every surfer dreams of—offshore peaks and minimal crowd. The forested cliffs of Royal National Park that end at Stanwell Park gave the area a feel of Kauai meets Carmel.

Later that afternoon, after checking out a surf contest at Sandon Point, we drove into an empty beachside caravan park in the village of Bulli Beach. We cooked up some lamb chops and passed out.

A few hours south of Sydney, the landscape changes from bucolic English-style pastures to Central America-like eucalyptus or "gum tree" rainforests and national parks. Our destination was Murramarang National Park, known for its population of "bodysurfing" Eastern grey kangaroos. The park is about forty-five minutes south of the surf town of Ulladulla.

The turnoff to Murramarang from the Princes Highway immediately transported us into the Lost World. The gum forest was thick, dark, and moist with heavy underbrush. A road sign warned of kangaroos. We spotted a lyrebird, a cross between a peacock and a turkey. Flocks of parrots flew across the road.

We arrived at Pebbly Beach and set off down the tree-covered path to a tree-lined cove. Daniel raced ahead. Israel and I arrived at a grassy meadow above the beach and found him surrounded by a mob of kangaroos. Daniel sat motionless, grinning from ear to ear, as a joey approached and almost plopped into his lap.

After we set our bush camp at the nearby Depot Beach campground, Israel stumbled upon a swamp wallaby feeding in the dunes. He described it as "a cross between a kangaroo and a giant rabbit."

Between surf sessions at a nearby reef, we hung out at our camp under a huge eucalyptus. We were surrounded by kangaroos and laughing kookaburras. At night, a pair of brushtail possums, nocturnal marsupials, nosed around our campfire in their nightly hunt for food.

Back in San Diego, the lives of my two rambunctious sons revolve around school, surfing, skateboarding, and water polo.

Living in a cramped VW van presented a unique set of challenges. Because Israel moved around like a worm in the upper van bed during our first night, he was exiled to a waterproof and sturdy Sierra Designs two-man tent. Daniel and I split the upstairs and downstairs van beds.

The boys quickly adapted to life on the road. Each evening after a day of surfing, they slapped steak, lamb chops, or hamburgers on the gas-powered campground barbie. They used their extra energy, during downtime in the van, to give me a surfing makeover: they hoped to improve my hopelessly out-of-date '70s flow surfing style. "Dad," Israel said. "You really need to work on your snaps. You aren't getting vertical enough."

An epic north swell we enjoyed during our stay at Murramarang had dropped off so we packed up the van and headed down the two-lane Princes Highway on our way to Bells Beach. The boys were exhausted from their last surf session.

Daniel gets close to a kangaroo, Murramarang National Park

We had communed with kangaroos and had become enamored of the beautiful coastline, abundant national parks and wildlife, excellent waves, and friendly people of southeast Australia. As we drove off, each of us looked forward to more surfing, more wildlife, and meeting more Aussies.

Chapter 19
PENGUINS, WAVES, AND WOMBATS

Phillip Island sits almost due south of Melbourne in southeastern Australia. To get there, we drove our rented diesel VW pop-top camper van through the immense coastal wilderness and ancient gum forests of Eastern Victoria or East Gippsland. The only other vehicles on the hilly two-lane Princes Highway were huge logging trucks filled to the brim with giant eucalyptus. The burned out hillsides and blackened stumps were evidence of the devastating wildfires that hit Victoria six months earlier (one hundred and seventy-three people lost their lives in January–February 2009 from the wildfires).

Managed by Phillip Island Nature Parks, a nonprofit organization established by the State of Victoria, the island is a Disney-fied version of a national park. It is home to a large colony of penguins, thousands of fur seals, wallabies, koalas, and a Grand Prix racecourse. Just a short drive over a bridge from the mainland, Phillip Island is one of the most popular tourist destinations in Victoria. Despite that, it is still ruggedly beautiful and has a variety of great waves for surfing.

Upon our arrival, we headed to Cape Woolamai, the most popular of the island's surf spots. The waves that broke along the beach, which is protected by large dunes, were shoulder high and immensely rideable. The water was in the mid 50s and required us to wear neoprene booties and hoods along with our winter wet suits. After about ninety minutes in the cold water, we returned to the van for hot tea, ramen noodles, and our hoodies.

During our stay on the island we scouted for waves during a succession of never-ending storms, offshore winds, rainbows, sunshine, and a hailstorm. We were in the middle of the Southern Ocean winter with weather coming straight at us from Antarctica. The boys and I enjoyed an afternoon of overhead Woolamai waves and then watched a squall snuff out our fun. Israel and Daniel found diversion from the rain in a maze theme park conveniently located next to our campground while I enjoyed a few rare hours of solitude.

Israel and Daniel at Bells Beach

The highlight of our stay on Phillip Island was observing hundreds of Little penguins (the smallest specie of penguins, about sixteen inches tall) emerge from the ocean in a "penguin parade." The penguins mesmerized Daniel as they emerged from the surf and waddled their way from the beach into their sand dune dens. We also enjoyed wandering among koalas and wallabies at the Koala Conservation Centre near our campground.

We pulled into Torquay, Australia's "surfing capital" and home of Bells Beach, one of the world's most renowned surf spots, with high expectations. The Santa Cruz-like city, about an hour southwest of Melbourne, is home to the Surfworld Museum and corporate surfing giant Rip Curl. The location for the longest running professional surf contest, Bells sits on a world-class reef just outside Torquay.

"Maybe we'll see pros here, Dad," Daniel said excitedly as we drove the Surf Coast Highway, passing surf shop after surf shop: Globe, Rusty, Quiksilver, and the large Rip Curl retail center. We hurried through town, found the turnoff to Bells from the Great Ocean Road, and drove by fields filled with kangaroos. As we pulled into the parking lot of the world's first surfing reserve, we could see that the swell was up. The surf at Bells, a vast reef and point fronted by sandstone cliffs, was not that good. Winkipop, a rocky point next door to Bells, where waves break for over a hundred yards, was firing. Israel jumped out of the van raced to the edge of the cliffs, and shouted, "It's going off!"

Over the next few days, we shuttled between the thirty-acre beachside Torquay Foreshore Caravan Park (that charged us about seven dollars a night for a campsite) and the Bells parking lot. After surf sessions, I cooked up pancakes and ramen noodles in the van.

The boys enjoyed meeting other visiting surf pilgrims from Tasmania, Western Australia, New South Wales, and Queensland, all living in their own beat-up vans, plastered with surf stickers, in the parking lot.

When we weren't surfing, we took day trips. An outing along the Great Ocean Road provided an introduction to one of the world's most scenic coastal drives. We took an overnight trip to the Twelve Apostles, a national park featuring awe-inspiring sandstone monoliths at the edge of the Shipwreck Coast.

We also enjoyed visiting the excellent Surfworld Museum in Torquay. The boys loved the Bells surf contest trophy "Bell," the huge display of retro surfboards, and the informative exhibit on the history of big-wave surfing.

One afternoon while surveying Bells from the parking lot, we could see that the surf was stormy and double overhead. Israel threw on his wet suit and rushed into the surf. I waited and paddled out with Daniel, who is more cautious. Together we managed to catch a few of the gray-black waves, enjoying the company of a handful of friendly locals who were ripping.

Back in the parking lot, after changing out of our wet suits, we realized that it was really cold. For the first time during the trip, the boys convinced me to get a motel room. We retreated to the reasonably priced Torquay Tropicana Motel near the Surfworld Museum, owned by Troy and Casey Dunlop, a young couple completely in tune with the needs of traveling surfers. The lobby came complete with a surfboard signed by world tour surf pros including world champ Mick Fanning (that sealed the deal with the boys). Troy, a surfer, promised a dawn patrol with offshore winds the next morning, and we slept soundly.

After another great surf session, we departed Bells the following afternoon and headed back north toward the warmer beaches of New South Wales. We enjoyed another month of surfing and wildlife adventures in Australia, including a great week with Emily exploring beautiful Jervis Bay. I couldn't have asked for a better place to commune with nature, spend time with my family, and explore one of the world's wildest coastlines.

Chapter 20

BASQUE BARRELS: FRANCE

There is a photo in a 1978 issue of *Surfer* in the article, "France: A Vintage Year," by surf explorers Kevin Naughton and Craig Peterson that has been stuck in my head since I was thirteen. It shows a man sprawled on a bench in the Basque village of Guéthary in France looking over a perfect blue-green wave peeling into an empty channel. So I was elated to find myself in exactly the same spot as that iconic image. Just like in the photo, the waves were pumping.

I was in France to introduce my sons to the country of my father, whose family still lives in and around Paris. The boys flew over with their grandpa first. After they spent a wonderful couple of weeks in Paris and the French countryside, I flew over to accompany them on a surf trip to the Basque Country, the center of the European surf scene.

After arriving in Paris, I spent a couple of days enjoying the Champagne Country, where my uncle has a house. There the boys and I loaded up a 2002 Renault miniwagon with our surfboards and camping gear. My cousins Vincent and Margaux accompanied us. After an uneventful eight-hour drive, we arrived in Guéthary, which is precariously perched above Parlementia, the wave I had longingly daydreamed about. At the Basque Surf Company Pro Surf Shop in Guéthary, I rented a six-foot-eight epoxy fun board and met shop proprietors Romo and Esteban, both longtime locals.

"Parlementia is the Sunset Beach of France," said Esteban, who grew up speaking Basque in Guéthary and was of mixed Spanish and American ancestry. "It is going to be big tomorrow, about eight to ten feet."

The following morning the sets at Parlementia were overhead. The boys and I caught a few waves with a father and son from Sweden and then paddled in as the wind came up. Later that morning, we checked out Alcyon, a grinding left that is best at low tide. Israel paddled out and caught a few lefts. "It was super shallow and the takeoff was super tight," said Israel. "Some guy yelled at me in French, and I had no idea why."

The next day the wind was offshore and the waves were pumping. The sets at Alcyon were in the six- to eight-foot range. Across the bay, triple overhead peaks broke over the Palmentaria reef, reminding me of the Tijuana Sloughs. I snapped a few photos of the boys and then paddled out to Palmentaria.

Waves were breaking over half a mile from shore. Big peaks came out of deep water and heaved across the reef. An eclectic crew of locals and visitors were out on big-wave guns. I was completely undergunned on my rental board. I managed to catch a few of the smaller set waves (I couldn't paddle into the larger ones). I ended the session happy that I had the chance to surf a spot I had wanted to surf for more than thirty years.

On our last surf day in the Basque County, we headed to the coast north of Biarritz near Hossegor, where miles and miles of empty beaches provide sandbanks with empty barrels. The world's best surfers assemble here each fall to compete in the Quiksilver Pro France.

The boys and I popped over the sand dunes of Le Penon in the village of Seignosse. The waves were overhead and offshore. "It's firing," said Daniel.

Israel broke his board on a stand-up barrel. At low tide I found a sandbar spitting out A-frames. One other surfer joined me.

"Is it normal to have an empty lineup on a Saturday afternoon in the middle of summer?" I asked him in French.

"Not really," he said. "But enjoy it."

So I did.

Israel at Hossegor

Chapter 21

BASQUE BARRELS: SPAIN

There was swell in the water. It was just a matter of finding a sheltered corner of Bahia de la Concha in San Sebastián in order to surf the stormy conditions.

"Dad, there are waves breaking in the river," Israel said as we drove past the Rio Urumea. "It looks like the entrance to Mission Bay when it gets big."

I was with Israel, Daniel, Vincent, and Margaux. With a base camp at a campground just across the French-Spanish border near Biarritz, we decided to spend the afternoon surfing and savoring the cuisine of San Sebastián, one of Europe's culinary capitals. "You almost can't find bad food in San Sebastián," said Esteban of the Pro Surf Shop in Guéthary.

The waves looked good at a little headland that divides Playa de la Concha from Playa de Ondarreta, west of downtown. "Let's get out there," said Israel.

Israel and Daniel shared semiclosed-out beach break waves with local kids. I took photos from the boardwalk above, where a parade of well-dressed tourists and local residents—or Donostiarras—as they call themselves in Basque, strolled by. The Basque name for San Sebastián is Donostia.

On the other side of the point, bodyboarders rode waves that bounced off the rock and high tide and mutated into an ugly Wedge-like ogre of a barrel. The waves pummeled the boys when they tried to bodysurf there.

That evening we ate delicious seafood *tapas* at a bar in the Parte Vieja. Scores of bars and restaurants in the old quarter play host to tourists who flock to the tiny cobblestone streets of San Sebastián each summer.

The next day, we headed to the fabled seaside village of Mundaka, located east of San Sebastián. Ranked the eleventh best wave in the world by *Surfer* magazine, Mundaka is a perfect left point that used to be a stop on the ASP World Tour.

Mundaka

I first surfed Mundaka back in October 1983 at the age of nineteen, when I was a UCSD undergraduate spending a semester at the Complutense University of Madrid. I took the overnight train from Madrid to Bilbao and caught a bus to Mundaka. As the bus rounded a curve along the highway that follows the Ria Guernica to Mundaka from Guernica, I caught a view of offshore waves peeling down the point. A few minutes later I jumped off the bus, left my gear with an Aussie camped out in the town plaza in a VW camper van, and paddled out. The waves were perfect.

I didn't expect it to be as good this time. But with a swell running, I figured the surf would at least be okay. As we passed the same point where I had first caught a glimpse of Mundaka surf twenty-eight years earlier, the boys spotted the lineup.

"It is perfect," said Israel.

Israel and Daniel surfed hollow lefts with a small crowd of very territorial and unfriendly locals. I surfed for a bit, tired of the crowd, and retreated to a local café with a great view of the waves.

The boys joined me for lunch. As they devoured giant *bocadillos* and surveyed the beautiful harbor and peeling waves, Daniel said, "It was crowded, fast, and perfect. I can't wait to come back."

Chapter 22

TUBES AND TAPAS

The *tapa* or *pintxo*, with its gelatinous and vegetable covering, looked delicious. Since the bartenders in this historic district Santander bar are typically rude, if not downright hostile, I didn't bother asking what the ingredients were. My initial taste caused me to gag and push away the plate.

"You know that gelatin is made from pig's feet," laughed Robert Amasuno, our guide and a longtime local surfer.

The last time I was in Santander, located on Spain's gorgeous and green Cantabrian northern coast, was in the fall of 1983, when I spent a few days surfing on a trip with my little brother, Nick, and my mother. We took the ferry from Plymouth to Santander on our way to Meknes, Morocco, where my dad was working on a United Nations project. Back then, the coast around Santander offered up empty waves, warm water, and just a few local surfers. The food was excellent. I'll never forget eating rabbit at a rustic country restaurant.

Today northern Spain is a vastly different world than it was thirty years ago. In the early 1980s, ETA terrorists exploded car bombs and carried out assassinations. Northern Spain was far from prosperous. The industrial north was bleak and filled with rows of working-class apartment buildings. Due to the recent crash and burn of the Spanish economy, rows of abandoned vacation condos litter the coast. South Americans, who immigrated to Spain when the economy was booming, fill many of the service jobs (back then it was the Spanish who emigrated all over Europe in search of work). Back in the 1980s, there were few surfers in Spain. Now surfers populate northern beach cities.

Despite the changes, northern Spain still has a rustic charm. The massive Cantabrian range provides a rugged backdrop to the green coast. Hikers enjoy the wildlife and scenery of the rocky shoreline. Picturesque cafés and restaurants serve up fresh and delicious seafood.

I was in Spain with Ben McCue and Zach Plopper of WILDCOAST, who had spent a college year abroad in Santander a decade ago. We attended the Global Wave Conference in Biarritz and San Sebastián, and were anxious to score world-class Spanish surf.

The second day of the conference took place in San Sebastián at the ultra modernist Kursaal Conference Center designed by Rafael Moneo at the west end of La Zurriola beach. When we arrived the surf was firing. Double overhead offshore waves broke at the west end of the beach. Bigger bombs to the east went unridden.

The minute the conference ended at the end of the day, participants grabbed boards, stuffed themselves into wet suits, and paddled out for an evening session. Soon surfer-conservationists from South Africa, Spain, France, England, Japan, Portugal, Australia, and the US shared plentiful peaks and hooted the best rides. After our surf, we assembled at the seaside People Café and Lounge on the *malecón* overlooking La Zurriola to sample *pintxos*, *jamón serrano*, San Miguel beer, and Rioja wine. It was a great ending to an inspiring conference.

The following day, Zach, Ben, and I drove to Mundaka. Near the historic city of Guernica, the once-dreaded *Guardia Civil* were out in force with machine guns manning a highway barricade in search of a Basque terrorist. From the ancient port at Mundaka, it appeared that about every surfer from northern Spain was out. I paddled out anyway, caught a couple of waves, and paddled in. The waves weren't worth the crowd.

At a bar overlooking the epic lefthander, Zach, Ben and I ate *bocatas de tortilla de patata* and admired the framed photos of pro surfers who competed in Mundaka when it was an important stop on the ASP Dream Tour.

"We'll hit up this cool little beach we love to surf that is on the way to Santander," Ben said.

"It should be firing and offshore," said Zach. "When storms move in from the north Atlantic, the wind on the north coast of Spain can turn offshore for days."

An hour later I looked out over at an empty wild beach. Offshore peaks broke in the distance. Soon after, I was surfing ultra fun A-frames. After our surf we found a nearby café and dug into bowls of *pulpo* and *calamar*.

The author at Dunas de Liencres Natural Park   Photo: Zach Plopper

In Santander we joined up with Robert and shared *pintxos* and *cañas de cerveza* at a nearby pub. "Tomorrow, it will be pumping," he promised.

Robert was spot on. The following morning I stood on the cliffs of Dunas de Liencres and watched aqua-colored offshore peaks. Sandbar peaks broke up and down the empty lineup.

"Most of the time in the winter I surf here by myself," said Robert.

A week later after I had returned to California, I received an e-mail from Zach: "Yesterday we scored Rodiles, Mundaka's little, yet hotter, sister. We have been blessed with two weeks of offshore south wind and swell."

Chapter 23
A COLD WATER HAVEN IN CANADA

As I arrived at Chesterman Beach, one of the most popular surfing beaches on Vancouver Island, I wasn't sure how the cold would affect me. The ocean and air temperature were in the high 40s. As I paddled through the whitewater to catch fun shoulder-high peaks, the cold didn't seem that bad. The lineup was empty except for Pete Devries—Canada's hottest surfer—and four of his friends, who all ripped. Devries pulled off big airs and slashing roundhouse cutbacks.

I joined the crew and was greeted with smiles and friendly waves. I was even given a wave or two. After a while the cold made it hard for me to get to my feet. I caught a wave in and found Emily on the redwood-fringed beach. A bald eagle circled overhead. Snowcapped mountains were in the distance. The scenery alone made the bone-chilling surf session worth it.

Emily and I were on Vancouver Island so I could give a talk at the 25th Annual Pacific Rim Whale Festival. Between surf sessions, we walked the desolate beaches and forests of Pacific Rim National Park and wandered the streets of Tofino, a former fishing and logging town that *Outside* magazine named "the best surf town in North America."

At the Wildside Grill in Tofino, Emily and I scarfed down

delicious salmon tacos, fresh seafood chowder, and the best salmon burgers I have ever eaten. Commercial fisherman Jeff Mikus and surfer Jesse Blake, who is also the chef, are the proprietors of

Wildside. I traded Mexico stories with Jesse, who had just returned from surfing Guerrero and Michoacán.

The following day, after I surfed empty offshore head-high surf at Wickaninnish Beach in Pacific Rim National Park Reserve, Emily and I ate fresh salmon at the rustic and surf-themed Shelter in Tofino. The great food and views of snowy peaks behind Tofino Inlet were a treat.

The view toward Jensen Bay, Tofino

After my talk, I paddled out at Wickaninnish expecting mellow overhead waves. Instead I realized that I had underestimated the size and power of the swell. The powerful sets were well overhead. Once again Peter Devries and his pals were out ripping.

After I caught a few peaks, the cold water found an entryway between the sleeves of my wet suit and my gloves. By my third wave, I was frozen. My body was shutting down. Back on the beach I was humbled by the ability of local surfers to rip in such frosty conditions.

As I drove over a snowy pass to catch the ferry to Vancouver, Emily said, "This is one surf destination I could come back to."

With a gorgeous national park, lots of wildlife, sumptuous seafood, and great waves, Vancouver Island has it all.

Chapter 24

UP THE 101: A COLLEGE SURF TOWN TOUR

I f you're the parent of teenage surfers in California, you already know your kids have no interesting in attending expensive and overrated universities on the East Coast. Thankfully California has the country's best public university system and more than few campuses are close to great waves.

To give Daniel and Israel and idea of the tough campus choices they would have to make—La Jolla, Santa Barbara, San Luis Obispo, Santa Cruz, or Berkeley—I drove them up the coast of California on a college and surf town tour during Thanksgiving week. Israel had just started thinking about college applications and SAT prepping. Daniel was along for the waves. Our plan was to visit UC Santa Barbara, Cal Poly San Luis Obispo, UC Santa Cruz, and UC Berkeley if we had time. The boys and I were to join Emily at my brother's house in San Francisco for Thanksgiving.

Ventura was our first stop before an afternoon tour of UC Santa Barbara. Israel and Daniel were determined to surf in the footsteps of Dane Reynolds, who made the hollow beach breaks of his laid-back hometown world famous. Israel had once surfed with Reynolds. "I even talked to Dane," Israel said. "He was so cool and was shredding."

Emma Wood, one of Dane's favorite local spots, was small.

Oxnard was a better choice. A-frames broke up and down the half-mile-long beach. The surf more than met our expectations.

Our next stop was Santa Barbara, the Monte Carlo of California. Santa Barbara is so luxurious that it makes Laguna Beach—its sister city in upscale shoreline chic—seem shabby. The beachfront UC Santa Barbara counts surfer-singer Jack Johnson as alum. At the end of our tour, we checked out Campus Point, UCSB's own surf spot. A few students enjoyed knee-high waves. "This place is awesome," said Daniel.

Israel and Daniel surfing San Francisco

We spent the night in the quaint fishing town of Morro Bay. The next morning, the boys and I shared overhead peaks at Morro Rock for a couple of hours. Afterward, we joined a crowded tour of the bucolic Cal Poly campus at the northern edge of San Luis Obispo.

At the end of the visit, Israel and Daniel spied the student "craft room" that doubles as a campus do-it-yourself surfboard-shaping factory and instructional classroom. "I can't believe you can make surfboards here," said Israel. "That's it. This is where I'm going."

That night we bunked at a seaside motel in Pacific Grove near Monterey in order to dawn patrol one of the kelpy local coves. Unfortunately, dawn revealed wind chop on the water. So we headed to Santa Cruz with a stop at Moss Landing to check out the sea otters in Elkhorn Slough.

After a tour of the redwood-lined campus of UC Santa Cruz, where we spotted a deer and a student we knew from the lineup in Imperial Beach, I drove downhill from the campus to Steamer Lane. The Lane, a world surfing reserve and ground zero for Northern California surf culture, is a frenetic hive of surfers, waves, street people, and surf-gazing tourists.

A new swell had just hit. The waves were overhead and pumping. The boys gleefully jumped off Lighthouse Point and into the Slot. I carefully walked down the upper staircase and threaded my way through rocks into the lineup at the Point. While I fought the crowd for a few lined-up rights, the boys snagged set waves at the Slot.

After our session, we hurried northward along the Pacific Coast Highway. Our destination was Half Moon Bay and Pillar Point, home to Mavericks, one of the world's premier big-wave surf spots. After I found the Mav's parking lot at the base of Pillar Point, the boys jumped out of the car to run down to the point along a trail that meandered through a grassy field.

"Hey, Dad," yelled Israel as he ran back to me. "That's Greg Long," he said, pointing to a lone surfer walking down the trail carrying a big-wave gun. Greg is one of the world's premier big-wave surfers.

"The waves are coming up," said Greg. "It's not super big. I wanted to get ready for tomorrow when the swell is supposed to be bigger."

The rocks, waves, paddle-out, sharks, and boils at Mavericks make it one of the most dangerous waves in the world. Mark Foo died surfing Mavericks in 1994. We joined a group of Japanese surfers on the cliff above the point to watch the sunset. The surf looked menacing.

Over Thanksgiving, between meals at my brother's house near the University of San Francisco, we scored waves at Fort Point under the Golden Gate Bridge. The day after Thanksgiving, Ocean Beach blew offshore all day and the surf fired.

The boys refused to tour any more college campuses.

———

Israel commenced classes at Cal Poly San Luis Obispo in the fall of 2014.

Chapter 25
BEYOND THE GOVERNMENT IN MEXICO

The campaign poster on a wall in Tijuana of Mexican presidential candidate Enrique Peña Nieto—referred to as "Bombón," or Eye Candy, for his preppie good looks—displayed the candidate grimacing while awkwardly hugging a much shorter, darker, Indian-looking woman. The odd ad might be the only kink in Peña Nieto's seamless campaign about nothing that is designed to earn the trust of Mexican voters who have forgotten the economic disasters and semi-authoritarian rule the Institutional Revolutionary Party (PRI) imposed upon Mexico for more than seventy years.

The specter of the return of the PRI to Los Pinos, Mexico's White House, is the reason that the polls show leftist candidate Andrés Manuel López Obrador, who is called AMLO for short, closing in on Peña Nieto, who until recently had a commanding lead (Josefina Vázquez Mota, the National Action Party [PAN] candidate is given little chance of winning). The victory of either Peña Nieto or AMLO on July 1 would mean a new but uncertain chapter in Mexico's evolving transition to democracy. Both front-runners represent Mexico's semi-authoritarian past in which the state plays a key role in the economy, press, culture, and everyday life with little or no oversight and accountability.

Although the twelve-year rule of Presidents Vicente Fox and Felipe Calderón, who governed under the mantle of the PAN, was a victory for the expansion of electoral democracy and the rise of a more robust civil society, it failed to create a political culture of transparency. Calderón's war on narco kingpins has been a tragedy and a failure.

In my own frequent forays into the bustling cities and forgotten corners of rural Mexico to promote coastal conservation, the bedlam of the narco war and absence of government is a sharp contrast to the entrepreneurial people I encounter and work with who are carving out a new Mexico that represents the emergence of an authentic civil society. This has resulted in a new optimism and sense of purpose that is propelling Mexicans forward to identify and solve their problems without asking permission of the once-omnipotent government.

While in Acapulco to host the BLUE Ocean Film Festival, more than thirty people were murdered prior to and during my stay. As a result, I assumed that our free film screenings would be sparsely attended. So I was surprised to find the restored art deco cinema in the city's seaside plaza packed with working-class families and beach lovers. Parents and their children sat rapt at the beautiful films and eagerly joined an open forum afterward about solving problems of beach pollution and coastal access.

In the Chontal indigenous village of Barra de la Cruz in Oaxaca, I met with residents fending off proposals to turn their coastline into a walled-off fortress in which they would be unwelcome guests. "We aren't interested in development," Pablo Narvaez, a fiery and articulate community leader, told me. "We are only interested in receiving training to help us run our eco-businesses. If we have strong businesses, we'll have a strong community."

In Tijuana, the city's new beacon of hope is chef and surfer Javier Plascencia, the proprietor of the elegant yet unpretentious Misión 19. While eating lunch with Javier recently, I was struck by his quiet and determined focus to create something new in the face the dark forces that should have caused him to flee his hometown.

Javier's pride in Tijuana and his driven creativity is changing the face and fate of this once embattled but now secure border city and inspiring a renaissance in music, art, architecture, and gastronomy in Baja California and throughout Mexico.

It is the boundless enthusiasm and passion for life that I encounter in Mexico that will sustain our southern neighbor beyond the inadequacies of the current slate of presidential candidates. That is why so many Mexicans, although outraged at what they perceive to be the media-engineered campaign of Peña Nieto or the old-school paternalism of AMLO, are buoyed by their fierce desire for normalcy and the realization that *"papá gobierno"* is now an absent parent that always seems to let them down and lead them astray. Their future depends on staking out their independence from the government that has little connection to the ordinary citizens who make Mexico a marvel of contradictions, chaos, and energy.

Chapter 26

THE BAJA RENAISSANCE

"I surfed K-38 last week," said Javier Plascencia, the chef and proprietor of Tijuana's Misión 19. Plascencia is from Tijuana, attended high school in San Diego, and grew up surfing both sides of the border.

The Tijuana surfer, along with fellow chefs such as Diego Hernandez of Corazón de Tierra, Benito Molina and Solange Muris of Manzanilla, Miguel Angel Guerrero of La Querencia, Flor Franco of Convivia, and brothers Javier and David Martinez of Boules and Muelle 3, are leading a gastronomic revolution in Baja. This renaissance is bringing the endemic and earthy colors, tastes, and textures of Baja's land and sea into what was the mostly moribund and touristy cuisine of the peninsula.

"Baja is undergoing a virtual renaissance now with a renewed interest in the region's gastronomy, culture, eco-adventures, lifestyle, and unique accommodations," said Jim Pickell, CEO and founder of Baja.com, a Baja-based company dedicated to helping travelers enjoy an authentic Baja California experience.

This new renaissance and revival of the authentic in Baja is an important and much needed antidote to the ongoing doom and gloom reporting on Mexico that has convinced many Baja fanatics to stay away from the peninsula. But due to the amazing things happening in the kitchens of these chefs, there has never been a better time to head south across the border.

My first trip to Baja was in 1967, when I was three. My mother and I joined our Los Angeles neighbors, a Mexican-American family, on a weekend trip to Ensenada, where we rode horses on the beach. When I was eight in 1973, we traveled to San Felipe, swam in the Gulf of California, and admired the majestic Sierra de San Pedro Mártir.

After I started surfing at the age of 13 in 1977, I spent a lot of time surfing the coastline between Tijuana and Ensenada. Those quick trips turned into longer expeditions with my father and friends to central Pacific Baja in a beat-up olive green 1964 six-volt Volkswagen van. We found friendly fishermen, pristine beaches, and perfect waves.

When Emily and I lived in San Ignacio Lagoon during grad school, Maria Luisa, a fisherman's wife and daughter, would lead Emily and me on low-tide hunts for octopus. The elusive creatures hide in the empty shells of *callo de hacha* or hatchet clams. Maria Luisa would use a metal hook to pry the shells out of the tidal flats. A couple of hours later she would serve *ceviche de pulpo* in the dining room of her plywood shoreline house.

I flashed back to Maria Luisa's *pulpo* when I sat down with Plascencia at Misión 19 in Tijuana's modern Zona Río and ate grilled *pulpo* with pistachio and garbanzo. It was delicious.

One of the other signature dishes of the new Baja Med cuisine is sashimi. "The only time I ate sashimi in Baja," I told Javier, "was with the fishermen of Punta Abreojos."

Once after being hit by the painful barb of a big stingray, I shared plates of fresh yellowtail sashimi with fishermen friends under a *palapa* in Estero el Coyote, a mangrove lagoon midway between San Ignacio Lagoon and Punta Abreojos. That fresh, sustainable, and globally influenced meal is the foundation for Baja Med cuisine.

When Baja hit rock bottom during the Great Recession and was plagued by narco terrorism, I could never have imagined that a group of inventive, creative, and visionary chefs would lead Baja out of the darkness and into a new world. The gastronomic renaissance in Baja and the creative energy that it has unleashed is something you cannot afford to miss. Because for the first time, the authentic taste of Baja is not just found in fish

Javier Plascencia, Tijuana

camps and rustic ranches. Now it is found in the revolutionary restaurants of Tijuana, Ensenada, and the Valle de Guadalupe.

Chapter 27
AROUND THE CAPE

The turquoise waters of the Sea of Cortez came into view on Baja's East Cape. A pod of humpback whales breached offshore.

"We're almost to Cabo Pulmo," said Cecilia Fischer, the WILDCOAST Cabo Pulmo coordinator, as we drove down a rutted dirt road to the tiny fishing village that abuts a 17,571-acre coral reef and national park. I was in southern Baja to give a talk to residents of Cabo Pulmo and the Cape Region to update them on the efforts of WILDCOAST to conserve the reef and the coastline that surrounds it.

A Spanish company, Hansa Urbana, has proposed building a new city larger than Cancún in the empty desert adjacent to Cabo Pulmo National Park. If the project is developed, conservationists and marine ecologists fear the reef will not sustain the impacts that are sure to come.

We arrived in the ramshackle hamlet of Cabo Pulmo and made our way to the Cabo Pulmo Beach Resort. "I first came here years ago," said Cole, the operator of the resort's Coral Reef Restaurant. "The reef was dead and the fish were gone. But now, diving the reef is incredible."

Back in 1999, local fishermen and the Mexican government brokered a deal to ban all fishing around the reef. The fishermen switched from harvesting the locally dwindling supply of fish to taking tourists to dive the reef. More than ten years later, researchers from Scripps announced the results of their decade-long monitoring project in Cabo Pulmo. The population of fish or "biomass" has increased 460 percent. Cabo Pulmo, they declared, was "the world's most robust marine reserve."

"We never used to see whale sharks here," Cole said. "Now this is one of the few places in the Sea of Cortez we can dive with them."

Humpback whale off of Cabo Pulmo   Photo: Ralph Lee Hopkins

Marine biologists and conservationists from around the world now visit Cabo Pulmo to learn about how Mexican fishermen helped to preserve a reef that is also a UNESCO World Heritage site. Renowned ocean explorer Sylvia Earle came to Cabo Pulmo to dive and named the Cabo Pulmo National Park a "Hope Spot."

After meeting with the residents of Cabo Pulmo, Cecilia and

I returned to San José del Cabo. The sprawling coastal city is a world apart from the desert solitude and emerald brilliance of the East Cape.

The next day I made my way through the bustle and traffic of Los Cabos on my way to Todos Santos. Emily and I lived in the artsy and historic village on the Pacific coast eighteen years earlier.

Todos Santos is still one of my favorite towns in Baja. It has great food, excellent surf, historic buildings, and art galleries. After surfing a beach south of town, I met up with Jim Pickell, who has an office in a renovated historic brick building. "Baja is back," he said. "Tourism is up and people are excited to come to Baja and rediscover the peninsula."

At La Esquina, an airy and friendly neighborhood hangout on the west side of town, I ordered a veggie panini and a carrot-beet-spinach-apple smoothie from Paula Angeloni, a local surfer. "I came to Todos Santos to surf," said Paula, who is originally from Uruguay and moved to Mexico to study marine biology in La Paz. "Now I'm raising my daughter here."

That evening I had dinner at La Dolce restaurant in San José del Cabo. The owner, Ramiro Rivas, a native of Mexico City, moved to Baja more than eleven years ago. When Ramiro is not working at his Italian restaurant just off the plaza in San Jose, he dives Cabo Pulmo. "I love Cabo Pulmo," he said. "It is so beautiful."

Over the next couple of days I dawn patrolled Costa Azul. The waves were small, but the water was warm and crystal clear. At the San José del Cabo farmer's market, I ate the best pizza in Baja and was delighted with the *vampiros*, giant quesadillas stuffed with portabella mushrooms.

"The farmer's market started out pretty unofficially," said Jim Tolbert of Baja Books and Maps, who hosts a stall in the market each Saturday with his wife, Judy. "Now we're a nonprofit. Thousands of people come here each week."

On my last evening, Cecilia and I drove out to the East Cape again. Our destination was the Crossroads Country Club at Vinorama where owner Joan Hafenecker has built a hotel and restaurant with an open patio that has savory food and an incredible view of the coast. After giving a talk to a collection of locals and visitors, wrestler turned Minnesota governor Jesse Ventura walked in with his wife, Theresa. No one even batted an eye. Everyone was too busy watching the sunset and looking for humpback whales to pay attention to a celebrity. It was a sublime ending to a perfect day on the cape.

Chapter 28

MIRACLE AT CABO PULMO

C abo Pulmo, a ramshackle seaside paradise inhabited by friendly fishermen and a colorful group of expatriates, is ground zero for efforts to restore the ocean. In Cabo Pulmo, local fishermen are working with biologists, conservationists, divers, and the Mexican government to protect a marine reserve that is a global model for the protection of an ocean ecosystem and fisheries.

I traveled to Cabo Pulmo to review efforts to defend the reef from the Spanish company Hansa Urbana that has proposed building a new city larger than Cancún nearby. My colleagues and I discussed future strategies needed to improve the protection of the coral reef that is home to humpback whales, sea turtles, manta rays, schools of giant fish, and a growing population of sharks, including the elusive and docile whale shark.

"There really is nothing else in the Gulf of California like Cabo Pulmo," said Dr. Octavio Aburto, a research scientist at the Scripps Institution of Oceanography who has studied the reef for years.

"Before there was a park, the reef and fish at Cabo Pulmo were not doing well," said Judith Castro, the daughter of a fisherman and a longtime resident.

The Castro family has lived in Cabo Pulmo for generations. But by the early 1990s, the fish were disappearing. There were fears that coral bleaching would forever damage the reef.

I first visited Cabo Pulmo in 1996 as the founding director of the Nature Conservancy's Sea of Cortez Program. Back then I worked with local conservationists and the Mexican government to try to manage the newly established national park at Cabo Pulmo. Due to local political conflicts, our effort initially failed. Marine biologists who had studied the reef and advocated for the development of the national park to save it were desperate. It took a few years, but by 1999 conservationists, fishermen, and the Mexican government came together to support a no-take reserve at Cabo Pulmo. Local fishermen, including the Castro family who had fished the waters of the region for decades, agreed to give up fishing inside the park boundaries.

"Our family had to learn to dive," Judith said. The Castro family now runs a successful dive operation.

Ten years later, Aburto and his Scripps team confirmed fish had returned to Cabo Pulmo in record numbers. "Fish biomass increased 460 percent over a decade, but even more critically the predator population increased over one 1,000 percent," said Octavio. "Abundant predators are key to healthy marine ecosystems. No other marine reserve in the world has shown such a fish recovery. There are so many fish that species like tuna are coming from outside the reserve to feed around the reef."

Even sharks, whose worldwide slaughter and decline has alarmed marine biologists and conservationists, have returned to Cabo Pulmo. "You can stand on the rocks at the end of Bahia de los Frailes at the western end of the reserve and see schools of sharks swimming around," said Sofia Gomez of WILDCOAST.

With additional recent good news from California's central coast about the increase in marine species in marine protected areas, there is reason to be hopeful that we can reserve the decline of the ocean. I hope that the success of Cabo Pulmo will inspire marine conservation efforts elsewhere.

———

In June 2012, former Mexican President Felipe Calderón cancelled the Cabo Cortés Project. However, in March 2014, a consortium of Chinese state-owned development companies announced plans to build a new city of up to 400,000 residents called Cabo Dorado, near Cabo Pulmo. That project was cancelled after conservation groups including WILDCOAST campaigned against the project.

Chapter 29

SURFING THE SUPERMOON

"Let's dawn patrol tomorrow," I said to Daniel as we watched sets pound Zippers and the Rock as the sun set behind us and the supermoon rose over the ocean. Dawn patrolling was our only way to escape the aggressive crowds. Surfers party hard in Cabo and aren't always awake at sunrise.

We were in San José del Cabo to attend a wedding during the same weekend as the Los Cabos Open of Surf. The contest meant lineups throughout southern Baja were full of talented surfers.

Daniel and I spent the previous afternoon on the East Cape surfing with Garrett Parkes and Matt Banting, two Australian pros. We shared rippable two- to four-foot rights with the Aussies, who gave Daniel a clinic in modern surfing. Daniel was elated. "Those guys really know how to ride these waves," he said.

We slipped into the ocean at the Rock before sunrise. With the moon illuminating the lineup, I spotted a jumble of sharp rocks sticking out of the water. I had not realized that the high tide the night before was followed by a very low tide the following morning. As we navigated the boils and rocks in the lineup, our dawn patrol was looking more and more like a bad idea. Daniel caught a head-high wave and kicked out at the last minute to avoid a rock.

"It's pretty sketchy out here," said Daniel, who wasn't happy about being woken up so early.

"But think of all the street cred you'll have by being able to tell everyone about your low-tide nighttime session at the Rock," I said.

Daniel wasn't convinced. "It is way too shallow. Let's paddle down to Zippers."

Once a Trestles-like wave that is still the epicenter of the Cabo surf scene, Zippers has been vastly reduced in scope due to the loss of sand from its once large beach. Adjacent development projects with their intrusive seawalls have turned what was the queen of the Cabo coast into a hit or miss wave at best.

As we paddled south the sun began to emerge in the eastern sky along with dreaded southeasterly winds. After catching a few bumpy rights and saying hello to shark researcher Dovi Kacev, we paddled in. Daniel returned to the condo and promptly fell asleep.

Later that morning the wind died and the Rock fired. Daniel and I paddled out and surfed great waves with no crowd. We finally scored in Cabo.

Daniel, East Cape

Chapter 30
SAYULITA

Sayulita, a coastal village in the Mexican state of Nayarit, is known for its artsy surf vibe and boutique- and gallery-lined streets. Invited to give a talk there, a short flight from San Diego to Puerto Vallarta put me into the capable hands of filmmaker Darrin Polischuk. "The surf should be fun," he said after I loaded my gear and my surfboard into his car.

Half an hour later, Darrin and I were surfing close to Punta de Mita, a green headland that forms the northern terminus of Bahía de Banderas. The tropical foliage and white sand beach reminded me of Hawaii.

"When we first arrived here a few years ago, we knew Sayulita was the place for us," said Darrin, who lives in Sayulita with his wife, Paulina, and two children.

After the session, Darrin drove through the rainforest on a small highway north to Sayulita. Upon our arrival in town, he dropped me off a few blocks from the beach at the brightly colored Petit Hotel Hafa, owned by Christophe and Marina Mignot. "Marina, the kids, and I came to Sayulita after traveling many years on a sailboat and living in Portugal," said Christophe, who is French. "We were looking for an easy living place with surf, sun, and culture. The family loves it."

The following morning, I walked around the corner from the hotel to the Café El Espresso Sayulita. After a shot of espresso, I walked down to the beach to check the surf. Fishermen readied their *pangas* and nets. Workers set up rental surfboards and umbrellas. With a Cardiff-like surf spot, Sayulita is the perfect destination for beginning surfers or surfing families. I first visited the town a decade ago with Emily and the boys. Israel had just learned to surf. "I got my first barrel in Sayulita," Israel remembered.

It was too windy to surf, so I walked over to meet Kevin Roberts of Punta Sayulita, who grew up in California and is developing an Indonesian-style residential village south of town. Kevin was the host for my lecture that evening and is the organizer of the Annual Punta Sayulita Longboard & Stand-Up Paddle Classic.

Later that day, Darrin picked me up again to search for surf, and once again the wind didn't cooperate. Just a few miles north of Sayulita, we turned into San Francisco (the locals call it San Pancho), an earthy coastal village that has become a new-age destination.

Huichol women in brightly colored dresses sold jewelry on the tiny *malecón*. Beautiful murals depicting the town's agricultural and indigenous legacy surrounded them. We visited the Entreamigos Community Center, a brightly painted brick building in the middle of town. Local children were reading in the library and busy with art projects.

"We focus on classes, lectures, art, community projects, and education," said Nicole Swedlow, executive director of Entreamigos. "The center was community designed, is community driven, and has become a gathering space and a place of tremendous positive energy."

After my evening talk on conserving Baja's coastline and a showing the documentary *The Baja Wave Document* at Punta Sayulita, I sat down to dinner at a restaurant on the town's colorful plaza with Paul Van Vleck, a photographer. Paul is a longtime friend from Coronado. We both lived in Todos Santos in the early 1990s. Paul keeps a small studio in Sayulita as well as a place in Puerto Vallarta. "I love it here," said Paul. "I have to live in Puerto Vallarta to work, but I come back as much as I can."

The following day prior to catching my flight home, Darrin drove me to another surf spot on the road out to Punta de Mita. After a short walk through a tropical forest, we emerged onto the beach to find waist-high waves and glassy conditions. Darrin and I shared waves with a few tourists on longboards and sea turtles swimming around the reef. It was a good omen and a great way to end my visit.

Chapter 31
INTO THE MANGROVES

Jose Antonio Oregon guided me into his *pango*, a wooden handmade pirogue covered with a coat of fiberglass and resin that he uses for fishing in Laguna de Potosi.

"A normal fishing skiff won't work here," he said. "The lagoon is too shallow. A *pango* has a flat bottom and gets us around better."

Laguna de Potosi, a twelve hundred-acre mangrove lagoon located south of the Zihuatanejo airport on the Costa Grande the Mexican state of Guerrero, sits behind nesting beaches for endangered leatherback sea turtles. During the winter, humpback whales swim in the sea outside the lagoon. In the summer, surfers visit to ride river mouth lefts.

Jose Antonio gently pushed the *pango* out into the lagoon. "There's a kingfisher," he said, pointing to the small bird with a large oversize beak darting across a lagoon channel into the mangroves.

My companions, Sergio Flores and Natalia Parra, know this coast well. They preserve sea turtles in Guerrero and attempt to halt the illegal trade in the meat and eggs of the endangered reptiles.

I was in Barra de Potosi to aid local efforts to halt a proposal by Mexico's National Fund for Tourism (FONATUR) to place a cruise ship terminal on top of the lagoon and the nine hundred-person ramshackle village. Barra was the first stop of the BLUE Ocean Film

Festival of Mexico, where ocean documentaries are screened free of charge for Mexico's fishing communities and coastal residents.

This small, friendly village of brightly colored fishermen's homes, sandy streets replete with handmade *terrayas* (throw nets), and numerous shrines to the Virgen de Guadalupe is the latest casualty in FONATUR's efforts to build megaresorts on top of some of the loveliest and most pristine coastal villages, coral reefs, and mangrove lagoons in Mexico.

"I don't see how they can build the project without destroying the lagoon and our village," said Jose Antonio, pointing to the colorful fishermen's *palapas* that line the nearby surf beach and the lagoon entrance.

Every weekend and especially during *Semana Santa*, Mexican families flock to the surfside *palapas* to pass the day eating sumptuous *ceviche de abulón*, *empanadas de pescado*, and grilled fish harvested from the nearby lagoon and sea.

Fisherman and his pango in Laguna Potosi

"Barra has some of the best seafood in Mexico," Sergio said. "It is a nostalgia trip for many of Guerrero's families who come here to spend time with their families and reconnect with fishing families they have known for generations."

The *pango* glided through a narrow channel lined with green mangroves that are home to more than two hundred bird species. We spotted blue herons, flocks of cormorants, night herons, and scores of kingfishers.

"Those guys are fishing for corvina and mullet," Jose Antonio said, pointing to a boat manned by two fishermen in broad-billed straw hats about a hundred yards out. The fishermen pushed their *pango* with a *palanca* or modified pole and paddle. They are Mexico's original stand-up paddlers. One of the fishermen balanced precariously in the *pango* and launched his *terraya*. Later we saw him perched next to the mangrove handlining for snook and pargo.

At a break in the mangroves, Jose Antonio led us over to a mud bank. We disembarked to visit a community salt-making operation. The salt makers use plastic sheets to hold lagoon water that is pumped into holding basins to accelerate the process. Piles of artisanal salt lined the sides of the salt pans.

Upon our return to the village, we greeted Araceli, Jose Antonio's sister and the village mayor at the *palapa* restaurant her family owns. Her mother, Linda, was preparing thick corn tortillas. A large pot of beans simmered on an adobe wood fire stove along with freshly caught red snapper.

"Have a tortilla," said Linda, handing me what looked like a pancake slathered with beans.

"We already lost the right to have our *palapa* here," said Areceli as we ate breakfast on a patio overlooking the lagoon. "And now FONATUR says that it has the right to deny our fishermen access to the sea. If they build their project, we'll lose everything."

That evening, more than a hundred of the town's residents

gathered in the street opposite the local elementary school to watch a selection of ocean films. Chairs line a sandy tree-lined street. We projected the documentaries on the school wall. Children received prizes for correctly answering questions about sea turtles and other ocean trivia.

"It would be a shame to lose this," said Areceli. Soon afterward, she flew to Mexico City to discuss the fate of her village and the lagoon with Mexico's media, elected officials, and government agencies.

I hope that that Araceli and her family and friends will be able to defend their village, the lagoon, and their way of life.

————

As of August 2014, the residents of Barra de Potosi had withstood the efforts to FONATUR to destroy the village, the lagoon, and their livelihoods.

Chapter 32

GIANT SEA TURTLES AND SURF IN OAXACA

Mazunte is a small fishing village about an hour north of Huatulco in the southern Mexican state of Oaxaca. Its white sand beaches and tranquil waters obscure its deadly past.

"Up until 1990, when Mexico banned the legal sea turtle fishery, more than two thousand sea turtles were killed each day in Mazunte," said Manuel Gomez, the congenial director of the National Mexican Turtle Center.

Today, Gomez and his team of biologists manage a beautiful sea turtle aquarium and museum, as well as conserve some of the world's most important sea turtle nesting beaches. "It is amazing to me that a little more than twenty years ago, fishing communities in Oaxaca that made their living from killing sea turtles are now protecting them," said Manuel.

I traveled to this unique corner of Mexico to hold an ocean film festival and meet some of the leaders who have made the sea turtle recovery and other coastal conservation success stories possible. I brought along my surfboard in the hopes of catching waves at Puerto Escondido and Barra de la Cruz. Mazunte was a stop on my way north from Huatulco to Puerto Escondido, where WILDCOAST was launching the film festival tour.

Known as the "Mexican Pipeline," Puerto Escondido is a balmy pleasant town that reminded me of Rosarito Beach in the 1970s. The beach at Zicatela, where swells funnel into shallow waters to create one of the world's heaviest beach breaks, is lined with *palapas*, restaurants, surf shops, and hotels. During south swell season some of the world's best surfers descend on Puerto to catch dredging barrels with elevator drops.

During our film festival event in the town's main plaza, two hundred and fifty people watched films and learned about the need to protect sea turtles. "We need to take care of our beaches," said longtime local surfer Roger Ramirez, who runs the Oasis Surf Academy along with his Uruguayan wife, Sol. Surfers in Puerto are fighting efforts to develop nearby Punta Colorada, a world-class bodyboarding beach.

In the morning I wandered down to Zicatela. The wind was offshore but the surf was tiny and closed out. "It needs to be a bit bigger," said Jason, a surfer from San Diego who knows Puerto well. "But there is swell on the way. Maybe we'll get lucky."

The next day I surfed a point south of Huatulco with a few local surfers and my WILDCOAST colleague Ben McCue. The first south of the season had arrived.

We drove to Barra de la Cruz, about forty-five minutes south of Huatulco, for the final leg of the film festival. Barra is the location of a perfect right point break and an important beach for the recovery of endangered leatherback sea turtles.

"You have time for a surf," said community leader Pablo Narvaez. "The sand isn't right yet for surfing. We need a few more swells to drag the sand from the beach out onto the point."

The community of Barra de la Cruz is managed collectively for the benefit of residents rather than for profit. The beach has been left undeveloped. Residents volunteer their time to staff a small surfside *palapa* restaurant. Surfers pay a twenty-peso fee to help maintain bathrooms with showers. Revenues from surfing pay for community health care.

Ben and I shared head-high waves with an eclectic group of local surfers and visitors from Brazil and Ireland. About an hour later, we met up with Pablo while we screened films for hundreds of children and their parents.

The next day the surf was even bigger. I caught a few hollow waves for a quick session before my return flight home, inspired by the beauty of Oaxaca and the determination of its people to protect their coastline.

Olive Ridley sea turtles off of Oaxaca   Photo: Claudio Contreras

Chapter 33
THE ROAD TO BARRA

The two-lane highway was endless. The drive from the pine-covered highlands of Oaxaca to the lowland jungle of the Pacific on the narrow and pothole and speed bump-filled road was made worse by the fact that I spent the night on a red-eye flight from Tijuana to Oaxaca. I was tired, cranky, and terrified that a bus driver or logging truck was going to swerve into my lane and force my rental car and me and my family off the highway.

Daren Johnson, a surf dad from Imperial Beach, followed. After ascending a misty mountain pass I expected a long, easy descent. I was wrong. Although we were only one hundred and thirty miles from Huatulco, we had another four hours of the windiest, curviest, scariest highway imaginable.

Members of Oaxaca's indigenous communities hiked along the highway that was lined with villages precariously perched among the pines along the steep cliffs. Women in traditional garb balanced their heavy loads on their heads. Others carried machetes on their way home from work.

Josh, Daren's son, was the first to vomit. Daren notified me via walkie-talkie that he had to stop. I found a slight turnoff on the wrong side of the highway next to a tree-covered deep ravine and pulled over. Daren followed. Israel immediately projectile vomited out the car window.

After three more hours of close calls with logging trucks and buses on what was in many places just a one-lane highway, we arrived in Huatulco. After purchasing supplies and groceries, we reached a bright orange beach house tucked away on a remote cove protected by rocky headlands on each side that was to be our base camp for the next two weeks.

Israel, Daniel, and Josh Johnson, Barra de la Cruz

The surf was head high and glassy. Daren, Josh, Israel, and Daniel claimed the thumping beach break peaks in the middle of the beach. I tried the point. The waves pitched quickly and unforgivingly. I was quickly reacquainted with the crunchy power of the surf in southern Mexico.

The next morning the boys surfed the point with groms from a nearby village. The swell had picked up considerably and the boys scored some epic and deep barrels. The sets were overhead and powerful. I cautiously dropped in on a few shoulders. The boys charged.

"Josh got a stand-up barrel," Israel yelled.

A set approached. I scrambled to get outside. Paddling into a wave, I dropped in. After riding down the line, I straightened out and caught the whitewater into shore. It was time to hit Barra de la Cruz.

At Barra, a beautiful rocky and sand-bottom point produces waves that wind down the beach in perfect cylinders. The subject of countless surf videos, Barra was the location of a Rip Curl Pro Search professional surf contest. Consequently, the village and beach is now packed with surfers from Germany, Austria, Israel, Portugal, Ireland, Brazil, France, Australia, and the US.

As we pulled up to the beach at Barra, I could see waves peeling down the beach. The boys jumped out of the car, grabbed their boards, and ran down to the point. The endless drive down the never-ending highway had been worth it.

Chapter 34

MUD PITS AND JUNGLE TRAILS

T he woman balancing a basket on her head patiently waited for Daren to make a decision about which fork in the road to take. Only one would take us to the point. Daren asked her in broken Spanish, "Where is the beach?"

"That way," she said, pointing to the right, still balancing the basket on her head. So we swung right and drove through wash bordered by pigs and two oxen yoked to each other.

We soon came upon a small pond covering the road. I wasn't about to risk losing a rental car by driving through it. I figured it was better to walk barefoot through the black, smelly water that likely harbored snakes, horse poop, clouds of mosquitoes, squishy stinky mud, and sharp sticks than risk getting a rental car stuck in the pit.

While Daren and I evaluated our chances of driving through the mud hole caused by Hurricane Carlotta, Josh, Daniel, and Israel ran through a trail in the mangrove forest and crossed the dunes to the beach to see if there was any surf. About fifteen minutes later they returned out of breath and sweating.

"The surf is flat," said Israel. "Let's go somewhere else."

"If we go somewhere else it's going to take us hours to find waves," said Daren. "Let's surf here."

We parked the car on the only dry spot we could find; loaded our backpacks with food, water, and sunscreen; took off our shoes; and hiked barefoot through the pond and another mile of swamp, mangroves, and dunes.

Soon we caught sight of the point and were rewarded with perfect overhead waves peeling for over a hundred yards and not another surfer in sight.

The clarity of the water made it easy for Daniel to spot a sea turtle. "I was paddling out," he said. "Something popped its head out of the water. At first I was scared but when I realized it was a sea turtle. It was super cool." Josh, Daniel, and Israel later swore they saw a large tiger shark.

At the end of the day, we trudged back to the car in the boiling afternoon sun. "Let's remember next time to spend a bit more time checking the surf before we write off a spot," Daren said. "We might have missed out on the best session of the trip."

We stopped by a local beachfront *palapa* for a dinner of freshly caught shrimp and perch. The local Chontals built the *palapa* in the hopes of attracting tourists to eat the seafood they harvest from a nearby lagoon.

"We want to protect our lands," said Miguel, a community member. "Our goal is to also create Mexico's number one sea turtle nesting beach."

Olive ridley sea turtles nest on the point we surfed and the beach fronting the *palapa*. Sometimes more than 25,000 arrive in one night to lay their eggs. More than 450,000 turtles lay their eggs annually.

On the way back to the main highway, I stopped and gave a ride to a farmer. "There isn't much work here," he said. "Everyone is returning from being in *El Norte*. There is not that much work there either."

The next day we decided to scout a point that is only accessible by boat or a long walk from a small village. I asked Esteban, the proprietor of a beachfront restaurant, about hiring a guide. "No problem," he said. "I'll find someone."

By the time we had our boards and backpacks ready, a young man jogged over to the car. He wore shorts, a long-sleeve rugby shirt, a baseball cap, and was barefoot. "I'm Pedro," he said.

As Pedro led us down the beach toward a rocky headland, the sun was scorching and the humidity was overpowering. Pedro started jogging.

"Aren't you hot in that long-sleeve shirt?" I asked Pedro, trying to keep up.

"I crossed the desert in Arizona during the summer on my to Washington State," he replied. "This is pretty easy."

The boys scrambled to keep up as Pedro ran up hills through the forest. Iguanas and squirrels ran away as we rambled down the trail. With my long legs I was barely able to keep up with Pedro. The boys fell behind. After about forty-five minutes, we arrived at a giant pile of boulders. "The waves are down there," said Pedro, pointing to a point. "Just climb down the cliff."

I did not want to risk injury by sliding down the rocky precipice. "We'll paddle around the point, Pedro," I said, pointing to a small cove that would require us to paddle around the headland. The paddle seemed less sketchy than sliding down a rock face into the lineup. We left our gear with Pedro, who promised to carry it down a longer trail to the beach.

The waves were small. While the boys and I surfed, Pedro patiently threw out his fishing line from atop the boulders. After a couple of hours we were ready to return.

On the way back, after showing us a spot on the beach where poachers raided sea turtle nests, Pedro ran back to the village through the dense forest. An hour later, drenched in sweat, we were elated to find head-high high offshore peaks breaking in front of the village. The boys paddled out while I made arrangements with Esteban to cook up freshly caught fish for lunch.

Three local kids out surfing were happy to have company. Very few traveling surfers visit the village whose residents depend on government farm subsidies and occasional employment protecting nesting leatherback sea turtles. I gave some wax to one of the local kids.

"Thanks," he said. "We don't usually surf with wax on our boards."

Esteban waved us in so we could eat the fish, beans, rice and coconuts he prepared.

On our last day, a swell hit. Daren and I padded out with the boys after dawn at the big sand bottom point. Overhead barrels reeled down the beach.

After about an hour, storm clouds appeared and it poured with rain. Nervous about lightning, we paddled in and huddled next to a cliff on the beach. Luckily the lightning was far off over the ocean. After the rain stopped, tens of thousands of large-winged brown insects appeared on the beach. They were followed by hundreds of terns that flitted above us, feeding on the insects.

After a few rolls of thunder, the storm clouds moved south. The sun came out and the insects and birds disappeared. It was time to surf.

Epilogue

S unrise. I stand on the rocks at Calafia in northern Baja, and wait for the nonstop Hurricane Marie-induced waves to subside. The surf is much bigger than it seemed from the top of the cliff in the gloomy darkness of dawn. My desire to surf the biggest south swell in twenty years is kept in check by my fear of being pummeled by powerful hurricane waves.

The set finally ends. I jump into a narrow gap between the rocks and paddle outside. I'm on my eighteen-year-old custom aqua Electric Duck eight-foot-one mini-gun that has propelled me through many memorable swells in Baja. I hope it has at least one more session left. Zach Plopper, who accompanied me on the predawn drive from San Diego, is somewhere down the beach ripping in the early light. He launched into the surf without any hesitation. Despite scraping his surfboard over a rock, he managed to barely scramble out before a fifteen-wave set blasted the point.

I make it to the top of the point and spot a set approaching. I paddle over the first wave. The second wave, a monster, explodes in front of me. I duck dive, wait for the impact, and resign myself to the deep. When the force of the whitewater hits me I wrap my arms and legs around my board as tightly as I can. I tumble underwater for what seems like minutes but is probably only a few seconds. I pop up and the third wave of the set blasts me again. The air is knocked out of me. I clutch my board like a lifeline. Finally I am clear. The ordeal is over. I climb back on my board and paddle back out.

After that, everything was easy. I figured out the pattern of sets that were swinging wide and outside and managed to catch my share. It was a good start to what turned out to be a historic swell, with Newport Beach turning into California's version of Puerto Escondido.

But Hurricane Marie wasn't the same for me without my family surf team to share waves with. My once plucky, skinny, little groms are now almost as tall as me and aren't always eager to surf with Dad. Israel, now a California State lifeguard, surfed early back home that morning (and broke his second board in a week), and then had to register for classes at Cal Poly. Daniel, who is also a state lifeguard, had just returned to high school after a long summer break. Luckily, I had surfed the hollow waves of Hurricane Lowell with them a few days before the Marie swell. I relished the session and realized how lucky I have been to share so many adventures and surf sessions with the boys before they needed to break away from Dad and explore on their own.

Besides, there is no shortage of ethereal coastlines to explore while the boys are in college. I've already mapped out some of the destinations—Iceland, Nova Scotia, Newfoundland, Chile, Argentina, British Colombia, Norway, Scotland, Ireland, England, France, Spain, and Portugal—that Emily and I can visit. Hopefully not too far off in the future, I'll be on a lost coast somewhere with Emily, the boys, and our grandchildren.

With the forecast of rising sea levels and dramatic changes to coastlines as a result of climate change, it is critical to explore, preserve, and enjoy the wild ones that remain. Our future depends on it.

About the Author

Photo: Jeff Wallis

Serge Dedina is the author of two previous books, *Wild Sea: Eco-Wars and Surf Stories from the Coast of the Californias* and *Saving the Gray Whale*. He is the cofounder and executive director of WILDCOAST an international organization that conserves coastal and marine ecosystems and wildlife. The Surf Industry Manufacturers Association named Serge the "Environmentalist of the Year" in 2003 for his work to protect the coastline of Baja California. In 2009 he received the San Diego Zoological Society's Conservation Medal. The California Coastal Commission and *Sunset Magazine* awarded Serge the "Coastal Hero" award in 2009 in recognition of his conservation work. Serge was named a UCSD John Muir College "John Muir Fellow" in 2013 for his contributions to conserving coastal environments.

Serge's conservation accomplishments include helping broker a deal to protect 140,000 acres at Laguna San Ignacio, a UNESCO

World Heritage site. Since then, he has helped to preserve over 400,000 acres and 150 miles of lagoon habitat and shoreline. Serge is now directing an effort to help the State of California manage and preserve a new system of marine protected areas in Southern California. He recently helped to stop a consortium of Chinese state development companies from building a new mega-city and resort next to Cabo Pulmo National Park.

The *Wall Street Journal*, PBS, the *Today Show*, *NBC Nightly News*, the *New York Times*, CNN, CBS News, *USA Today*, the *Washington Post*, the *Economist*, the *Los Angeles Times*, *Newsweek*, the *Boston Globe*, the *Christian Science Monitor*, and the *San Diego Union-Tribune* have reported on Serge's conservation activities. Serge has published articles on the environment and surfing in the *Los Angeles Times*, *Grist*, *Voice of San Diego*, *Network*, *Surfline*, the *Surfer's Journal*, the *San Diego Union-Tribune*, the *Surfer's Path*, *Journal of Borderlands Studies*, and *California Coast & Ocean*.

Serge holds a PhD in geography from the University of Texas at Austin. He received his master's degree in geography from the University of Wisconsin and a bachelor's degree in political science from the University of California, San Diego.

An avid surfer, Serge is a former State of California and City of Imperial Beach ocean lifeguard. He has lived, surfed, worked, and studied in El Salvador, Mexico, Peru, Spain, England, France, and Morocco. Serge currently lives in his hometown of Imperial Beach where he was elected Mayor in November 2014.